SUCCESS RITUALS 2.0

Winning Habits of High-Achieving Women; How She Does It and How You Can Too

Compiled by:
Gina Bell

IAWBO, Institute for Aspiring Women in Business Online
c/o Signature of Success Consulting Inc.
RPO Cathedral, PO Box 33081
Regina, SK S4T 7X2 Canada
www.IAWBO.com
publisher@iawbo.com

ISBN: 978-0-9866867-1-9

Published in the US, UK and Canada

Book Cover: Lorrie Miller Hansen

Interior Layout: Susan Daffron, Logical Expressions Inc.

Dedication

This book is dedicated to women
in business online who are inspired
to add value and increase to the
lives of others by doing the work
they love.

Your success illuminates
and expands every woman's
sense of possibilities through
entrepreneurship.

Let's keep the ripple rolling.

Contents

Introduction   1

Behind Every Successful Woman is Herself: Get Clear Grow Rich   3
Gina Bell

Feel the Shift. See the Results.   13
Laura West

The #1 Secret to Creating your Ideal Life   21
Suzanne Doyle-Ingram

Lessons from a Compulsive List Maker: How to Make One List
with a Purpose   31
Dawn Cullo

The Not-So Glamorous Secret to Success   39
Carla Young

A Satisfying Sunday and a Success Ritual You Can Do In Bed   47
Jennifer Bourn

One Size Doesn't EVER Fit All   55
Beth Sharkey Flarida

Does Success Begin With Being Wrong?   63
Britt Michaelian

Does Waiting for Lady Luck Bring Success?   69
Catriona Welsby

It's Time to Get Moxie   75
Crystal O'Connor

Be Happy And Passionate and Watch Your Business Soar!   83
Janet Majoulet-Foust

Seven Critical Rituals of Online Success to Increase Profits Now   89
Jenna Drew

Quantum Leaps in Life and in Business through the Power of
Conscious Creation   97
Jennifer Longmore

Defining Success and Understanding Me   107
Jennifer Urezzio

Client Attraction and Retention Rituals   113
Katrina Sawa

No Time, No Money, No Excuses: How to Create Part-Time
Success (In the Real World)   123
Kim Page Gluckie

Dump the Junk that's Holding You Back and Make Room for
Success   137
Kimberly Englot

What's the Point If You Can't Dance?   143
Kiva Leatherman

Taming the Chaos of Information Overload   151
Laura Lee Sparks

The Unintended Ritual (and a Few I Planned)   159
Kim Doyal

Building Wealth from the Inside Out with Affirmations   167
Linda P. Jones

5 Ways to Guarantee Success, Personally, Professionally and
Spiritually   173
Lisa Manyon

Relationships – The Heart and Soul of Your Business   179
Mary Kay Morgan

Creating Your Day By Design: A Daily Grand Ritual for
Massive Success   185
Nachhi Randhawa

A Simple System (and a Dirty Little Secret) for Completing
Monster Projects   191
Nika Stewart

Intention to Action: The Essence of Success Rituals   197
Patrica Selmo

Life and Business by Design   205
  Randi Pierce

Letting the Spirit Speak   211
  Sherri Garrity

Of Creatures and Habits   219
  Susan C. Daffron

Successful Moments to Be or Not to Be   225
  Tricia Dycka

Free Gifts from the Success Rituals 2.0 Co-Authors   233

Introduction

"An Apple a Day Keeps the Doctor Away" is an age-old health ritual with a simple message… eat something healthy every day to maintain good health.

What if this simple, sound advice could apply to more than just health?

What if it could apply to something like the success of your online business?

It can!

Inside Success Rituals 2.0 you will discover the winning habits of successful women in business online; surprisingly simple things, that when done consistently, can dramatically improve and maintain the health of your business and support long-term success.

Think of it this way… It's not what you think and do once in a while that makes the difference, it's what you think and do day in and day out.

And we want you to take it one step further…

By illuminating the winning habits of high-achieving women, my co-authors and I aim to inspire women entrepreneurs to become more aware of the success rituals that impact their success AND remind them of the one essential ingredient that makes a winning habit winning… that is taking consistent, daily action to realize new and extraordinary results.

As you read through *Success Rituals 2.0* you'll likely find chapters that seem written just for YOU. Pay close attention to them because you've attracted this book into your life for a reason.

Love & Success,

Gina

Gina Bell
President & Founder,
IAWBO.com

Behind Every Successful Woman is Herself: Get Clear Grow Rich

GINA BELL

"Learning new things won't help the woman who

is not using what she already knows."

— *Author Unknown*

I love this quote. It's a reminder of how frequently we look outside of ourselves for solutions, when more often than not; we already know or have everything we need to reach that next level of success.

Do you believe it? Most entrepreneurs don't – thus, the booming information marketing industry and entrepreneurs suffering and spinning in overwhelm. Maybe you can relate?

Are you ready stop the insanity? I sure am!

You see, the greatest impact of my work with women in business online is helping them a) become aware of their own ability to influence their success and b) get crystal clear – leaving no stone unturned. When this happens, breakthroughs are guaranteed. I call it The Clarity Effect.

When you get clear the how appears. Not by magic (even though it seems that way) but because clarity empowers you to make quick decisions. You don't have to spin anymore because you KNOW exactly where you're going and precisely what to do first and next.

If you want to see an immediate positive shift in your success, my best advice: get clear now.

Unfortunately that's not what most entrepreneurs do (I can tell you're not "most" just by the fact you're reading this book). Most entrepreneurs spend more time getting clear about their wedding or honeymoon or forthcoming holiday than they ever do about the business that is supposed to support the lifestyle they dream about.

If you're feeling like the direction of your business has taken on a mind of its own or you've started to lose that loving feeling because of overwhelm and indecision the great news is you can hit the refresh button - now. Clarity will be your launching pad.

To get you started, here are a few of my favourite clarity inspiring success rituals. They involve a lot of introspection because this is where big breakthroughs happen. Self-honesty is essential. Ready? Here we go:

Get Clear Success Ritual #1: Leverage hindsight to gain insight for future success.

I take a K.I.S.S. approach to everything I do which means, keep it strategically simple. One of the ways I love to teach new concepts is using acronyms. They are simple, memorable and actionable with easy to follow steps.

L.E.A.P. is an acronym that demonstrates how to transform hindsight into the insight you need to leap your success forward. I recommend doing this exercise at the start of the year and mid-way through. Give it a try:

L = Look Back and list. Looking back on the previous year make a list of what you believe worked and what didn't. Sometimes we move so fast we forget the actions that produced the best results. Or, we make a mistake that could have been prevented if we remembered that it didn't work the first time we tried it.

E = Evaluate your findings. Ask Why. Looking at what worked – why did they work? Looking at what didn't – why didn't they work? What lessons can you extract that will create positive change moving forward?

A = Affect future results by taking action. Determine exactly how you will apply your findings. What will you modify, change, eliminate, and add? Be specific and schedule these actions into your calendar (or your team's).

P = Prioritize and Plan. What are your next 90 day, 6-month and annual goals? Use your new insights to create your action plans.

Get Clear Success Ritual #2: Leverage what you already know

Successful people are committed to life-long learning but that doesn't mean they don't also leverage what they already know.

Before you purchase another product or enrol in that next program you have your eye on, here are a few questions to ask yourself:

1. What area of my business needs the most attention – right now?

2. Is this product or program I'm considering relevant to the current gaps in my business?

3. Do I need to develop additional skills or purchase new resources in order to address this area? (i.e. maybe you *know*

but struggle with implementation – actually doing it/getting it done)

4. Does it make more sense for *me* to learn these skills OR, does it make more sense to hire a specialist?

Make sure you're evaluating what areas of your business need attention – right now. Investing in these areas are the most applicable, provide the best ROI (return on investment) and will move you forward more quickly.

If you're continually investing in skills and resources that you "may need someday" rather than what will move you forward right now – you'll find you're not moving as quickly as you'd like. And that is SO frustrating!

Getting ahead of ourselves and investing in these products and programs we might need in the future is one of the top ways we self-sabotage – and, totally unnecessary.

Simply checking in with yourself before you buy (even if you choose not to) can accelerate your speed of success.

Keeping your feet on the ground in this way requires a level of self-honesty that I believe is essential to long term success.

When we consistently evaluate what we already know and are clear about the actions we can take or gaps we can bridge right now we are always empowered to move forward today and every single day. Inch by inch everything's a cinch.

Get Clear Success Ritual #3: Dress for Success (on the inside too!)

"Dress for Success" is common advice. It's an approach to being in and doing business that fuels great first impressions, boosts marketing confidence and more.

But, there's a catch that not a lot of people talk about…

The phrase has become so common that it carries along with it a preconceived definition which can ultimately take our focus away from the big picture.

Think of it this way…

It's like a coin sitting on a table. One side is facing up, that's how we know it's a coin but without the backside, the part of the coin that's not visible, the coin holds no value. It's not something we consciously think about.

If we use this analogy, the "other side of the coin" is your INNER image of success.

It's easy and commonplace to focus on the external stuff… hair, clothing, eye wear, handbags, website design, business cards, brochures, and on it goes.

But the reality is that there is a synergy that exists between our inner and outer image. One without the other impacts our success experience.

Synergy = the working together of two or more people, organizations, or things, especially when the result is greater than the sum of their individual effects or capabilities. The "things" in this case are inner image and outer image.

So the external stuff IS very important but becomes diluted if our inside isn't dressed for success too. I'm referring to our thoughts, intentions, goals, authentic definition of success and so on.

The typical entrepreneur invests major resources (time, energy, money) into the external image probably because it's the easiest to take action on, heck some of it can even be delegated… and even better, set it and forget it.

And avoiding it isn't the solution either because if that synergy doesn't exist and if one image is stronger than the other there's an imbalance that often manifests in the form of self-deception and sabotage.

You've either experienced it or witnessed it, the person who looks amazing on the outside, their marketing materials and website rock but they don't seem to be experiencing much success. And it's likely due to an imbalance because they neglected the other side of the coin.

So, here are five things you can think about and do now to make sure you have a balanced image (inside and out)…

1. **Define what success means to you.** Often we adopt other people's definitions unknowingly (usually the result of comparison) so it's really important to check in with yourself on this frequently.

2. **Clearly define where you (really) want to go.** What are YOUR goals? What are you striving for? Write down what you really want… both short term and long term. You have to know where you're going before you can get clear about how to get there. That sounds so logical yet so many entrepreneurs never gain the level of clarity they need to create the kind of business and lifestyle they dream about when they get started.

3. **Commit to Self-honesty.** It's astonishing how good we can be at self-deception. Pay attention to your self talk; to the excuses you make and to any discrepancies between what you say you want and what you're actually doing to get it. Are you more committed to the comfort of the status quo or the success you say you desire?

4. **Check in with your attitude and intention.** Whether we are discussing life or business, coming from a "what's in it for me" attitude is a relationship killer. Instead, think about how you can add value and increase to the lives/businesses of others. What goes around comes around. When you lead with

the intention of giving it's almost impossible to be perceived as salesy.

5. **Nurture positive thoughts.** Most people don't like to spend time with negative people; chronic complainers or bullies. Did you know that up to 80% of self talk is negative? Learn to recognize the truth in your self talk. The negative self talk is a natural reaction to fear – an attempt to keep you safe. Unless the fear is justified this natural tendency doesn't serve our quest for success.

So the next time you're focused on dressing for success on the outside, check in with your inner image too.

Your Brain is on Your Side (or is it?)

Finally, the #1 reason why I focus so heavily on clarity with my own success rituals and the work I do with my clients is because **it sets the law of attraction in motion.**

Clarity activates your Success GPS. Here's how:

You already possess a powerful tracking system that will guide you to all the things you really want. It's your Reticular Activating System or RAS for short. The RAS is an automatic mechanism inside of your brain that serves as a filter between your conscious and sub-conscious mind bringing relevant information to your attention and it plays a vital role in your ability to achieve goals.

Don't worry about the science; focus on what it does for you...

It's like wearing golf ball finder glasses. When golfers lose their golf ball in the underbrush, the technology of these cool glasses eliminates the light from background objects and makes the golf ball itself stand out. The relevant information is the golf ball, the golf ball finder glasses is your RAS.

If you've ever purchased a new (or new to you) car only to see a dozen of them on your drive home – that is a great example of your

RAS at work. Now that the make, model and color of the car is relevant to you – your RAS brings them to your conscious attention. You've probably driven past them a hundred times but never noticed them until today.

What's' really cool about your RAS is that you can deliberately get it working for you by choosing the exact messages you send from your conscious mind. The #1 way to do this is to get crystal clear about your goals – so clear that you can see them, feel them, taste them.

You've likely heard dozens of experts tell you how important it is to get clear and focused about your goals. Many of them probably even shared HOW to do it. Now you know WHY clarity is so darned important!

And it gets even better…

Your RAS cannot tell the difference between what is "real" and what is "imagined".

A great example here is Olympic athletes. Many professional athletes use visualization techniques to practice and perfect their performances before actually doing it. They know how to get their RAS working for them.

So are you ready to activate your success GPS?

The first step is to gain crystal clarity about what you REALLY want so that you have very specific vision of your goal in your conscious mind. Your RAS will then begin to filter all relevant information and bring that to your attention.

Opportunities and resources will begin to emerge – almost out of thin air. The reality is that your RAS is making you aware of everything that is relevant to achieving your goal.

See why I get so excited about clarity as a success tool? I love it!

And if you're loving it too you'll get my audio program "Clarity: The World's Greatest Success Secret" inside the Success Rituals 2.0 Virtual Goodie Bag at www.SuccessRitualsGifts.com

About the Author: *Gina Bell is The Laptop CEO at Gina Bell Inc and Founder of IAWBO, the Institute for Aspiring Women in Business Online.*

As a Freedom-Rich Business Architect™ Gina loves to teach high-achieving women how to create the freedom, flexibility and fortune they crave using a Simple Online Success Formula.

Get the Simple Online Success Formula Express Course, The Girlfriend Effect Special Report and Weekly Success Tips delivered by email free when you subscribe at www.IAWBO.com

Feel the Shift. See the Results.

Laura West

Your daily ritual for plugging in to
creativity and inspiration to get more of the
right things done

I have a multi-six figure business, which I run from my home office, two active athletic sons who keep me driving all over the city of Atlanta and beyond for tournaments and events, as well as a vibrant life of my own.

With this very fully life and busy schedule, I often get asked, "How do you manage to come up with such creative ideas, create so many programs and products, and just plain get so much done?"

My secret: I start every day with Creative Bagel Time.

Each morning I head out to a cafe somewhere nearby and start my day with a bit of reflection time, which I call Creative Bagel Time (CBT for short). It has become a life changing and business enhanc-

13

ing structure for me. It's truly the reason I get so much done – it's because I'm always shifting my energy and tapping into my highest wisdom and creativity.

I don't start my day by starting with the hard thing first. I start with aligning my energy with what I really want to create and then "doing" from there.

My clients have heard about this success ritual for years. I've been surprised at how many people want to know the details... what do I do, what do I bring, what do I wear, do I really eat bagels every day?

You too can create your own morning reflection time, and you'll be amazed at how your day changes – it's like plugging directly into inspiration and creativity.

Getting Started

The idea is to get out of your home office or your regular office environment for 30 to 60 minutes EVERY DAY.

I know, every day may sound challenging or even luxurious. It's not a luxury –it's a must! If you want your business to change and grow, then you have to do something different.

If you are skeptical, try it for two weeks and see what's possible!

The first place to start is you have to put your CBT time on your calendar. Block it off. This is non-negotiable time with yourself for you and your business.

Now What to Wear? You may wonder what this has to do with it. Managing your energy is everything. If you feel good about how you look, then you're already starting off with good vibrations. I'm dressed as though I'm engaged in life, and that's attractive to people.

I dress to make myself feel inspired, what I call "creative casual." I might dress up a little funky and fun or wear my heeled boots. Another day I'm in jeans and a fun coral colored suede jacket. I also check in with my energy and my plans for the day and dress accordingly. Do I need a boost in my energy? If yes, I don't slouch into my ultra casual clothes; I give my energy a flourish with accessories or great shoes. I always have more people talk to me when I'm looking good and feeling good. Beats starting the day in front of anonymous email!

Where to Go? Pay attention to the energy of your local bakeries, cafes, restaurants and coffee shops. Some cafes are lighter, darker, happier, calmer, busier, and the food fare is different depending on your taste for the day. Sometimes the more popular coffee shops aren't really set up for you to take up space for an hour at a table. Find somewhere you can comfortably set up your inspirational space.

What to Bring? The next step is to pack your Inspiration Bag. You want a bag on hand that is already packed with supplies, just like you're going on a mini-retreat each morning.

You want to pack your Inspiration Bag with all the goodies you need to get grounded and inspire creativity.

Here are some of my favorites:

Books – I might bring a new personal growth book or a long-time favorite. You just want to read a few pages to help you relax and get plugged into what's possible in your life and business. Some of my all-time favorites: *The Scarcity Trance* by Victoria Castle, *Spiritual Economics* by Eric Butterworth, *Law of Attraction* by Esther and Jerry Hicks, *Wisdom's Choice* by Kathleen Shapiro. I bring just one depending on my mood.

Magazines – Bring to browse through for inspiration. A few of my favorites: *Art Journaling Magazine, O, Body and Soul, Time,* and *Fast Company.* It doesn't have to be business-related. Anything that gets you inspired and feeling connected to possibilities will shift your energy, and then once you are plugged in, you can shift your creative focus to your business ideas.

Journals – I like to have two journals. One is my personal journal, and one is a larger notebook for my business ideas.

Find a type of journal you enjoy writing in. I personally prefer 5x8 spiral-bound with no lines. I want my journals to lie flat. There's nothing worse than not really being able to write on the pages of a journal because it won't open all the way. By the way, here is a reason to get out those beautiful journals people have given you… YES, you can write in them!

Pens and Felt-tip Markers - I love markers and the way they write so smoothly. They just flow on the paper so easily - I swear it helps the ideas to just tumble out when the pen flows! And then the colors… I'm not an artist, but using different colors makes me feel creative (that's half the battle, isn't it?) and lets the ideas come to life. I keep a little zipper pouch full of markers ready to go!

Ezines and Web Stuff - I print things off during the day and save it in a pile for my creative time. I write all over other ezines about my own thoughts and ideas, different perspectives, websites to check out, etc.

Laptop – Every now and then, I'll bring it along when I know I want to write a specific piece and need to be out of my office for the flow to happen. Everyone is a little different here. Mostly though, I find that I like to go out into the world, get inspired, and then come back and write on my computer. There is something really special about starting the day writing by hand; it's such a visceral experience.

Personal Energy Alignment

Now, what to write?

You want to start with your personal thoughts and ideas. This is the first step to align your energy. Sometimes I'm in a crabby mood, or I might be in an anxious mood because I have so many things going on. When this is the case, I just need to write in my journal to get things out of my mind. It's a catharsis. It frees up my mind to focus once I dump everything out. (Kind of like dumping out your purse and reorganizing, which feels so good!)

Here are a few other ideas:

Synchronicities - This is a favorite of mine. I write them every day. My world (and yours) is full of amazing things that happen. Phone calls, chance meetings, surprising websites, emails that contain exactly the right information you were looking for... This practice can be life-shifting! When you start noticing, tracking, and writing down evidence that the Universe is conspiring for your well-being, you will truly start to believe it. It will erase any doubts, and will support you in being more confident.

Gratitude - Another form of appreciation is to write a gratitude list. Just notice all the things you are grateful for in this moment.... warm beds, sunny husbands, cooperative children, laughs, hot coffee, French toast bagels. Your heart has an electromagnetic field 50 times greater than your brain, and expressing gratitude and appreciation will expand that loving energy. Imagine as you are writing that you are spreading love all around the cafe to everyone who comes in.... Now that's a way to start a day!

Morning Pages - Follow Julia Cameron's advice from *The Artist's Way*. She recommends writing three pages nonstop. I swear by this advice. Always, always, always by the end of the second page, I will tap into my inner wisdom, and some brilliant thought, idea or aha will surface. Even if I struggle at the beginning to write something, as long as I keep going, my third page will have some juicy insight or idea.

Now you are primed. You've shifted your energy, and you are ready to focus your creativity and inspiration toward a business idea.

Brainstorming Business Ideas

At this point, I get out my Marketing Notebook for brainstorming, ideation, rough drafts and "what-if-ing."

Heart Maps - This is my version of free flowing, no-rule, mind map. I take an idea that I'm stewing about or am getting near deadline, or it's an idea for an article or a new program. Put a topic in the middle of the page (maybe even turn your notebook sideways). Draw lines out like spokes on a bicycle (it's ok to be squiggly and messy!), and then put one thought or step about the center topic. For example, if I'm thinking about the CD recordings I'm doing, I'll put that in the middle page inside a quickly drawn heart. Then I draw spokes out to different questions, thoughts or ideas I have about the topic. "Who to interview?" "Design for a cover." "Write a recording agreement." "Get it transcribed." You don't have to write things in order; the idea is to get you out of your linear "in-the-box" thinking and just let your thoughts free-flow. You will be surprised at what you know. This allows me to expand out an idea and play with possibilities without having to start with a "to-do" list. Some areas for your heart map:

- Article Ideas
- New Programs
- New Products
- Launch Campaigns
- Presentations and Teleclass Design
- Email Messages

Once I've primed the pump by consciously shifting my energy and tapping into this creativity, then I'm ready to go back to my home office and get into action!

What's Next?

Before I leave, I create my Daily Giggle Goals for the day so I'm ready when I get back into my office.

From my brainstorming and idea-ing, I make a list of three things that I will focus on for the day. Three things that will have me smile, or even giggle at the end of the day because they moved me forward in my business. These Daily Giggle Goals are usually so easy to do because I've lined up my energy, I feel grounded and focused, and I know what's important.

When I leave the café, my energy is up. I am inspired. I'm grounded. I'm focused on what's important to me in the day. I usually have kickstarted my creativity on a business idea, and I'm full of enthusiasm to get it going.

It takes courage to start your day shifting your energy and tapping into your creativity. By committing to this daily practice I have totally transformed my business. I get projects moved from "great ideas" to "real life programs and products." And, the best part is that they are so spot on target with my ideal clients because I've taken the time to tap into my inner wisdom and channeled my creativity into a focused idea.

About the Author: Laura West is the President of the Center for Joyful Business and JoyfulBusiness.com. Ms. West attracts thousands of amazingly creative and committed business owners to her teleclasses, programs, retreats, products and workshops.

As a certified business coach, author and speaker, she has helped women around the world create successful businesses filled with spirit, authenticity and prosperity. She is also the author of the upcoming book, Awaken Your Inner Business Goddess *as well as the creator of several information products including: Business Goddess's Guide to Creating Powerful Sales Pages and the popular Joyful Business Guide™, a creative marketing plan for your business using law of attraction principles.*

Find Laura online at: www.JoyfulBusiness.com @JoyfulBiz on Twitter Facebook: http://www.facebook.com/JoyfulBiz. Step into your confidence, creativity, and power - download the free Business Goddess Manifesto at www.JoyfulBusiness.com/manifesto

The #1 Secret to Creating your Ideal Life

Suzanne Doyle-Ingram

If you were to describe your ideal life, what would it look like? What kind of house would you live in? Where would you live? What would you drive? What activities would your kids be doing? Where would you travel? How often would you travel?

Now take a minute to describe what it would cost you if you left these dreams unaccomplished. Would it cause frustration? Anger? Resentment?

And what would you need to do if you wanted to create this ideal life?

I'm going to tell you what the key is to fulfilling your goals and creating your ideal life, but first, let me ask you another question: What is your WHY? Why are these things important to you? For me, it's my three kids and my husband. I love the life we have and I love making it even better.

As a business owner, there's only one simple thing you need to do to create your ideal life.

Are you ready for it? Here it is: SELL.

That's it. Just sell more to your customers. Simple, right?

Look, I know what it's like to be working a ton of hours and making less money than you deserve. I've been there. When I started my first company, I wasted hundreds of hours trying to find a shortcut to success. And when I started my second company I made the biggest mistake of all which is very embarrassing to admit, but I'll be honest with you. I modeled my business on other unsuccessful businesses! Duh!

Finally, things started to change for the better as I read, studied and learned everything I could. I invested in a coaching program and my sales revenues rose higher and higher. I took a good look at what I was doing repeatedly in my business, and I developed systems to automate certain procedures. I learned to leverage my time more effectively. I figured out that I could work 60 hours a week to make $40k or I could work 60 hours a week to make $250k and once I got there, I could leverage my time so that I can work 30 hours a week to make even more.

One of my business associates asked me the other day with tears in her eyes, "Am I not working enough hours? Am I not working hard enough?" It's not about working hard. If that were the case, construction workers would be millionaires! It's just about selling more. Plain and simple.

I run two businesses now working 30 hours a week. One is a direct marketing list brokerage company with 5 full time employees and the other (which is my passion) is a business where I help women business owners learn how to "Sell more to their clients in a way they'll thank them for."

I'll let you in on another secret. I used to be afraid of selling. Yes, I'll admit it: I was terrified to sell! Here's what would happen: I hated cold calling and reaching out to anyone so I would hardly have anyone in the pipeline. Then, I was so grateful whenever I made a sale, that I wouldn't want to "jinx" it by offering an upsell! Have you ever felt like that? I was just terrible at sales. I used to sweat just thinking about it.

Then one day everything changed. I was the Director of Operations for ModernDog Magazine and the publisher suggested that I move into sales because she thought I'd be good at it. I remember being horrified at the thought of it and begging her, "Please, I'll do anything else! I'll wash your floors, walk your dog, I'll do anything but please don't make me sell!!" I'll never forget that day. She looked at me and said, "Aren't you proud of what we have here? Don't you love this magazine?" I did love the magazine and I was very proud of it. She continued by saying that people who advertise in our magazine get their product in front of thousands and thousands of dog owners. There are a limited number of spots that we can sell and once they're gone, they're gone. So if someone wants to take you up on the opportunity, that's great. And if not, there's always another person who really wants this spot. You just have to find them and connect with them.

Makes sense, doesn't it? Once I changed my mindset, my sales increased dramatically. I went from "desperate pursuer" to "opportunity-giver."

I have good news for you; you can add a few simple strategies into your current business and very quickly and easily increase your sales.

Here's how:

#1 Spend more time working on your IGA's (Income Generating Activities) and less time doing the non-essentials

Income generating activities are the things that you do to increase your sales revenue. For example, creating products or packages, negotiating with vendors/suppliers, selling in person, selling on the phone, and so on.

I encourage you to borrow my 30-30-30 Rule and adapt it to fit your business. We have a rule in our direct marketing company that our account managers must connect with 30 people a day (by email or phone); they must respond to a lead within 30 minutes; and if someone wants to place an order, they must write up the order within 30 minutes. If you connected with 30 people a day, either by email or on the phone (preferred), that's 600 people a month! How many of those would result in sales? How much would that mean to your bottom line?

Another important IGA is picking up the phone and calling your prospects and clients. Email is getting lost in the shuffle these days. Personally, I get over 400 emails a day so I often miss them. If you want to connect with someone, call them.

Think about your business and list the ways that you could sell more frequently to your customers. Could you offer incentives? Could you host a VIP event? Bring a friend day? Set up a recurring order? When I took a good look at my business and realized that I was only selling one thing to my customers one time, I knew that had to change. Think about some of the ways you could serve your customers more fully by offering them other products or services that they need. They will thank you for it!

Sending your prospects and clients a newsletter at least once a month is a "must-do". I know what it's like to be paralyzed by this one. I used to put it off, month after month, because I had no idea what to write about. Start a newsletter idea list in your notebook and every time you have an idea, write it down. Your newsletter can be very short – people appreciate that! You can mention industry news, upcoming events, emerging trends, and/or tips and strategies. It's vitally important to get your name in front of your prospects and clients at least once a month. Here's the key: Your prospects and customers do not know what you have to offer. They can't remember and you can't expect them to. Always remind them of what exactly you have to offer.

Sending your newsletter by email is the cheapest and quickest distribution method, but sending it by mail is more effective. I recently hired someone to write my newsletters for me. I give her the ideas that I want covered and she makes it sound great! I can pre-load them into my autoresponder and then forget about them for a few months.

I can't stress enough how important it is to outsource anything that can be done cheaper, better or faster by someone else. (More on this later under "Get Help")

#2 Set Goals and stick to them

I write down my goals on paper with a pen, never on my computer. I write down how many new clients I am going to get each month, what my financial goals are and what projects I am going to finish. Then I stick it on my wall next to my computer. It's so easy to forget about our goals if they're not right in front of our nose. Studies have shown over and over again that people who write down their goals are more successful than those who don't write down their goals. You can't just think about your goals, and you can't just "wing it" in your business if you want to be truly successful.

#3 Think like a matchmaker

Never push someone into buying what you have if it isn't the right fit and isn't going to serve them. Help them get what they need, even if it means going elsewhere and losing the sale. You will earn their respect and potentially earn their referrals. (This has happened to me many times. I have had 20 referrals from one person who has never bought from me!)

Get your head into your client's head and ask yourself how you can be a better match for them. What do they need from you? How can you give today?

#4 Get help

Stop doing time consuming tasks that don't make you any money. If I find myself doing something mundane like formatting a document, I will suddenly stop and outsource it right away. Heads of companies do not do minimum wage jobs. This takes time away from selling and increasing revenues.

Here's who I use for outsourcing:

- On Fiverr.com (www.fiverr.com) you can get someone to write an article for $5, tweet about you to their followers for $5, or write a press release for $5, you name it you can find someone to do it. Anything for $5!

- I have a Dedicated Assistant with AskSunday (www.AskSunday. com) who arranges appointments for me, updates my blog, books travel arrangements, and other tasks.

- Stop cleaning your own house! Hire a cleaner to come in and do the floors and bathrooms once every two weeks.

- I outsource my book keeping, my SEO, my back links, my web design, some of my writing (not all), my blog updates, and much more.

- In my house, we have someone to cut our grass, do the laundry, clean the house, make meals, fix things, and more.

Regarding hiring a housecleaner, I've met many, many women who say they can't find a cleaner who will clean to their standards. I used to feel the same way too. Then one day I had an epiphany. At the end of my life, how do I want to be remembered? That I was kind, generous, fun, a good mom… or someone who had really clean toilets? At the end of the day, it's all about choices. Don't let perfectionism paralyze you. Don't self sabotage by thinking that no one can do things as well as you. You will get burnt out eventually if you try to do it all yourself (ask me how I know this). Good enough really is good enough.

Yes, it costs money, that's true. But when I'm done work for the day, I can leave my office and go play with my three kids because Lisa's making dinner. I used to hate having to say to my kids, "Please get out of the kitchen, I'm trying to make dinner." Especially after I hadn't seen them all day long; they were clamoring for my attention and I was irritated because I couldn't give it to them.

I understand when you're not making very much money, it seems like a pie-in-the-sky fantasy to have someone making your meals for you but it really is attainable. You could put an ad in your local paper and hire a Mother's Helper for probably $15/hr. What if she came to your house three days a week from 3pm -6pm and watched the kids after school and got dinner ready? Better yet, what if she picked the kids up from school so you could continue to work uninterrupted? What would that mean for you? It would cost approximately $135 a week or $540 a month. Do you think with the extra 24 hours of work (from 3-5pm) you could sell a little bit more to make up for that? I know you could!

Not only would you increase your sales, having a Mother's Helper would absolutely change your life. Believe me, it's amazing what it does for your stress level. You could even ask her to prepare the kids' school lunches (or your lunch) for the next day - wouldn't that make your morning that much easier?

#5 Give your help freely.

Look for opportunities to help others. This investment comes back to you many times over. As business owners, we have a responsibility to give back to others. And this is especially important as you grow your business. You can help your clients by giving them information, articles, discounts, bonuses, special service, and much more.

You should also look for ways to help your fellow business owners and colleagues. Imagine if you went to them asking, "Is there anything that I can help you with?" Perhaps sending them a referral, or sending a special offer from them to your customer base. When you need help, and you ask for it, what's going to happen? They'll be there for you too.

Never forget the three most important characteristics of an entrepreneur. You must believe in yourself 100% (even when others are judging you). You must be extremely self-disciplined. And it's crucial to understand the urgency of Now – never put something off until tomorrow when it can be done right now.

The strategies I've given you are some of the tried-and-true things I've done to grow my business. I love helping women succeed in business and it gives me such a thrill to hear their successes. I encourage you to implement some of the above strategies to boost your sales. Even if you start small with one or two things. Don't allow it to be overwhelming. Start by connecting with 30 people a day. Then add a newsletter. Then add another product or service. You'll see a difference in your business and you'll be well on your way to creating the ideal life you've dreamed of.

Decide what you want, make a plan and take action. Happy selling!

About the Author: As an Accelerated Revenue Specialist, and also referred to as the "Revenue Rescuer", Suzanne Doyle-Ingram has a laser-like ability to see hidden sales opportunities for small businesses as well as the experience and wisdom to convert them into instant revenues!

Suzanne delivers high impact strategies to quickly and easily boost your small business revenues using proven and reliable sales techniques and systems. Discover how to ethically serve your clients more effectively (and make more money) in her books, workshops and tele-seminars.

Visit Suzanne online at www.SuzanneDoyleIngram.com and sign up for your free Revenue Boosting e-course today!

Lessons from a Compulsive List Maker: How to Make One List with a Purpose

DAWN CULLO

I am a recovering compulsive list maker. I used to make a lot of lists, I would make one list for my errands, one list for my chores, a daily tasks list, and a business task list, and it just went on and on. I became so wrapped up in making lists that it became an overwhelming chore. Then I read the book *Eat That Frog*, By Brian Tracy. In the book he describes various ways you can overcome procrastination, and basically you just need to start with your most difficult task, or your ugliest frog. I am not fond of frogs, so the many analogies made towards eating frogs made getting through the book tough. However, I did discover one great tip from his book that has really worked for me. The tip that I discovered was learning how to make one task list with a purpose, and this task list was also going to help me achieve my goals.

A task list with purpose is one that will help you accomplish your daily tasks as well as achieve your goals. This has helped impact my success because when I check items off my task list I know that I am closer to achieving my goals. For example, one of my business goals is to create a thriving Virtual Assistant firm. To create a thriving business I will need to get more clients and the only way to that is through marketing. Therefore, everyday on my task list I create a marketing task for my business.

Defining Goals

To make a task list with a purpose you need to first start by defining your goals. When you define your goals you are creating clarity and motivation in your life. You can't get anywhere in life without clarity. Once a goal is set then the motivation to complete that goal is what drives your daily success. Each time you check off a task you are one step closer to achieving that goal.

To start making your goals, find a place in your house where you won't be interrupted or lock the door to your office and put out a Do Not Disturb sign. Take out a sheet of paper and a pen to write out your goals. It is best to actually write them down on paper because the act of writing them down and seeing them on paper makes them tangible.

Each goal should have a clearly defined target end date because goals without an end date will just lead to procrastination. Below each goal write out a list of what you need to do to achieve that goal. Those items will now become part of your daily task list and help move you towards achieving that goal. Your goals should be personal and business related this will help to create a work life balance.

Creating Routines

When making your task list, it is best to not get caught up in creating a list full of household chores and errands. One thing that I found helpful was to create a cleaning routine for my house, a laundry routine and a specific day for errands. This helps contribute to my success because if I don't schedule a specific day to work on household chores I will end up cleaning the house for hours because I haven't clearly defined a starting and stopping point.

The cleaning routine is a tip that I picked up while working in the retail industry for a few years at The Disney Store. The store that I worked at was located in San Francisco and it was huge, at the time it was the largest store on the West coast. It was impossible to complete the cleaning tasks for the entire store before it opened. The management team created a cleaning routine for the entire store. Each day only one area of the store was dusted and vacuumed and this created a cleaning rotation which only took about 20 minutes per day to complete instead of a few hours.

To apply this technique in my home, I grouped together areas of the house that can be easily cleaned together. For example, on Monday the living room and dining room cleaned because they are right next to each other and are pretty easy to clean. I make sure to include the bathroom as well because no one likes to clean the bathroom so it is best to get that done on the first cleaning day. Then on Tuesday I tackle the kitchen and the office, Wednesday I clean the upstairs bedrooms and bathroom, Thursday is the master bedroom and bathroom and Friday is the playroom. To create a cleaning routine, walk through your house and figure out how you can group areas of your home which would be easy to clean together. If you have two story house, it would make sense to clean those rooms together and leave the vacuum upstairs for a few days.

The laundry is on a routine as well. I wash all the bed sheets on Tuesday, the kids clothes on Wednesday, casual items on Thursday and my husband's work clothes on Friday. When putting together a laundry routine, think about when the clean clothes will be needed. For example, I do my husband's work clothes on Friday because he has casual dress day on Friday and does not need to wear his normal work attire so it can be washed on that day. His laundry is done before the week starts and he doesn't need to scramble on Monday morning to find a clean shirt to wear. I still include all of these items on my daily task list so that I don't forget to do them.

The Task List

Now that you have made your goals and laid out your cleaning, laundry and errand routines it is time to start the next step of making your task list. Again, this task list should be well thought out, not just one that lists your daily chores. While those are important to your daily household goals they shouldn't be the only type of tasks on your list

The technique that helps me make the best possible task list is to make it before I go to bed. This is helpful because the house is quiet and I can actually have some time to myself to think clearly. Also, doing this activity prior to falling asleep helps to clear my mind and I have found that I actually sleep better when I make my task list before bed.

For each item on my task list I assign a number, either 1, 2, 3 or 4. The tasks with the number 1 are those that need to be done today. The tasks with the number 2 are items that I would be nice if they were done today but not critical, items that are number 3 are tasks that need to be done during the week and tasks with the number 4 are those I want to get done by the end of the month. If there are any tasks listed as number 2 and are not checked off by the end of the day then they are bumped up to a number 1 task for the next day. Look back over your goals list and the tasks that you wrote down to help you achieve those goals. Picks items from that list to add to your task list, continue this process each time you make your task list.

My Monday task list looks like this:

1. Workout

1. Clean Living room, Dining Room & Bathroom.
1. Wash and change all bed sheets
1. Grocery shopping
1. Write blog post about article marketing.
1. Follow up with Jessica
2. Listen to Teleseminar
2. Call Mom about Thanksgiving
2. Read 10 Pages of personal development book
3. Send in Scholastic Book order for Lily
3. Order Birthday gift for Abigail on Amazon
4. Research vacation locations

Your task list should be created on something that you can take with you and be able to look at several times during the day such as your cell phone. The reason for looking at your list several times a day is so that your tasks and goals are on top of your mind all day. Keeping up with your list on a daily basis takes a lot of dedication. When you are aware of your task list throughout the day you will achieve your goals faster because they are on top of your mind all day long.

Most phones have some kind of notepad program where you can list your tasks. I have the type of phone which has the ability to install applications. One of the applications is called Springpad. This application is great because it is a list making program that can be accessed on either my phone or on my computer. What I love about this is if I am working on my computer I can log into my Springpad account and check off tasks from my list and it will automatically sync with my phone. Having the list on your phone is a great idea because when you are waiting in line at the grocery store or sitting your car waiting for your kids to get out of school you can review your list.

You use your cell phone several times a day which provides you an opportunity to check your list throughout the day. If you put your list on a piece of paper it will more than likely just get tucked into a deep dark hole in your purse or coat pocket never to be found again.

Scheduling

Now that you have your goals defined, established your routine and your task list is done you can now schedule time to work on these tasks. To achieve your goals you need to carve out time in your day to work on your business and personal goals. I utilize Google Mail and Calendar to help me manage my life. They are viewable on my phone and instantly sync on my phone when I make a change to the calendar on my computer. I block off time in my calendar to work on my business, my home tasks as well as my personal development tasks. If I don't schedule these things in my calendar then I probably would never do them.

Once the kids are in bed I finally get some quite time and can sit and work for a few hours without interruption. The first thing that I do is review my task list and any items in number 1 that are not already checked off get worked on first. Then I look at my calendar to see what I should be working on next. I then wrap up by working on my task list for the next day.

In closing, remember to clearly define your goals as those will help guide your daily task list. Be sure to work on the hardest tasks first and keep up with your list every day and before you know it you will be achieving your goals and setting new ones.

About The Author: After a 10 years career as Administrative Assistant and "Go to Gal" in a traditional office environment Dawn decided to

open her own Virtual Assistant company so she could be the boss and still be that "Go To Gal".

In 2006 she began helping clients with their Microsoft Word and Excel projects. Following the Social Media boom her focus shifted to helping clients market their businesses online thru Facebook, Linkedin, Twitter, Blogging and Article Marketing. She has Internet Marketing Specialist and Social Marketing Specialist certifications from VA Classroom.

Dawn lives in sunny Northern California in the town of Rancho Cordova with two annoying cats, one husband and two amazing daughters, Lily (2005) and Abigail (2010). She enjoys Photography and spending time with her family. www.SunriseVirtualServices.com

The Not-So Glamorous Secret to Success

CARLA YOUNG

What I am about to share with you about success is not glamorous or sexy, it doesn't have the makings of the next Hollywood rags to riches story, and often, it isn't even that much fun. It's not even a magic bullet that will get you there in a single leap if only you purchase this one extraordinarily special program.

What it does do is get results: plain and simple.

What is the secret to success, you ask? What is the way less than glamorous not made for Hollywood and sometimes boring secret that will get you results? One word: consistency. That's it – just plain old fashioned showing up and getting it done.

A Little Story about Consistent Action

The first piece of advice I ever got in business was this: "Tell people what you do." meaning reach out to my network and let them know that I had started a business and ask for their support.

It sounded simple enough, except that my entire network consisted of two people (it was a very short day at the new home office calling them and letting them know what I was now doing). So 30 minutes into my business, my job was clear: meet more people.

That's exactly what I did. Week in, week out, I attended networking events, breakfast meetings, after work socials, corporate open houses. You name it, I was there doing my job: meeting people.

In that first year alone, I not only did I meet with over 1,000 people, but I followed up with every single one of them. From this network of connections, I built up a thriving consulting business where when a colleague asked his network who he should use for copywriting, 2 out of the 3 people who responded recommended me.

I followed the same simple formula in building my social media network. Every day showing up, engaging in conversation and meeting people. That consistent action allowed me to quickly build a social media following and grow my influence.

The same was true when I built the social media brand for a new online magazine for mom entrepreneurs. Every day I showed up and shared tips and advice using the company hashtag #MOMeo. Now when my followers wonder what to do to stay focused and motivated, they ask what would #MOMeo do (and I respond).

7 Golden Rules for Taking Consistent Action

Taking consistent action isn't always as simple as it seems. It should be, but we have a nasty habit of overcomplicating and cluttering the issue and just plain getting in our own way. Think of these as the golden rules for taking consistent action:

1. Shift your Mindset from DO-ing to Finishing

We are the great and powerful starters – the multitaskers capable of spinning plates while chatting on the telephone and soothing a crying baby. Or at least we think we are.

Doing isn't enough. Doing starts projects, but doesn't finish them. Doing makes task lists and starts on 8 of the 10 to-do's, but never checks ANY of them off. Doers have big ideas and goals that rarely get off the ground. Doing is not going to get you there and is the #1 enemy of consistency.

Shift your thinking away from doing because being busy isn't necessarily being productive. In fact, often sitting quietly and thinking is a lot more productive than frenetically flittering around your task list like a crazed hummingbird.

STOP doing and start finishing because 90 percent done is still not done.

2. Build a Sunday to Friday Work Routine

It's easy to get overwhelmed or lose focus, especially when the week starts rolling (or rather steamrolling us) with unexpected tasks and distractions. Without a routine to fall back on, you are dooming yourself to failure.

Routine is the simplest way to get in the habit of consistent action. Think of it as the autopilot routine you fall back on when stress and overwhelm start to pull you out of your daily rhythm.

Create a standard Sunday to Friday work routine template in your calendar by giving each of your work days a core theme and try as best as you can to stick to that daily theme.

For example, start your week with 30 minutes of prep time Sunday evening. Designate Monday as your Get Stuff Done day to set the tone for your week. Tuesdays and Thursdays are client and/or project work days. Wednesdays are a meeting day. Friday is a wrap up and metrics day.

3. Focus on the 'Right Things'

To say that all you need is consistent daily action would be a little misleading. If consistent action were enough, you could flap your arms three times a day and call it good. What matters is consistently doing the 'right' things.

So what counts as the right things, you ask? That's why golden rule #3 is all about creating a priority measuring stick to measure activities and opportunities against your goals and objectives.

For example, common priorities for all businesses are earning money and generating sales leads (that lead to future money). Applied to a consulting business then, your focus should be client projects (billable time) and connecting with potential clients. That's it – plain and simple.

Write out a list of your top three 'right' things and paste it on your wall. Whenever considering a task or project, ask yourself which one of the three right things it brings you closer to. If the answer is none, move it to the bottom of your daily action list.

4. Build your Self-Awareness

Sometimes when we least expect it, fear and self-sabotage sneaks into the picture and messes everything up. The reason it is so dangerous and worthy of discussion in a chapter on consistency is it disguises itself as action.

It's called busy work. The simple definition is the unimportant tasks and projects we pursue when avoiding the work that will move us forward (closer to achieving our objectives). It's important to recognize the signs and symptoms of this type of self-sabotage before it halts our momentum.

Most often we have favorite busy work activities (or distractions) that we turn to when we start feeling overwhelmed. Examples are checking and rechecking email, hanging out in social media socializing or tidying up your office.

Make a list and when you find yourself spending too much time on your busy work distractions, simply stop, ask yourself what you are avoiding and move on to that task.

5. Take Daily Action FIRST!

Good intentions are one thing, but following through is quite another. That's why your daily work routine is as important, if not more, than your Sunday to Friday work routine because let's face it – shit happens.

Start your daily work routine with high priority tasks. The reason is twofold – #1: Your energy and motivation levels are much higher first thing in the morning and #2: Distractions and crisis's tend to come up later in the day.

Get in the habit of starting your day by accomplishing at least one core objective before checking in. That means no email, no voicemail, no social media – just you sitting down and getting it done.

6. Measure your Results!

The reason is simple: what gets measured, gets managed. Results are not only the best gauge of your activities, but an amazing motivator and reinforcement of consistency (remember how I said it sometimes gets a bit boring?).

Knowing that what you are doing is getting you results will help you avoid the temptation to try the latest and greatest glamour marketing tool or follow a me-too fad down the vortex of wasted time and energy. The easiest way to stick with what works is knowing that it works.

Know what you are aiming for, break it down into key milestones, and track your metrics on a daily, weekly and monthly basis.

Based on your metrics, adjust your daily action steps accordingly by dropping what isn't working and focusing on what is getting results.

7. Create Support Systems

Some days, consistent daily action is going to be easy and other days, less so. Life happens, family members get sick, technology fails or any number of countless outside forces get in our way.

That's why you need to create support systems. Think like a Boy Scout and always be prepared with backup childcare, a sick day work plan and so on. Consistency doesn't happen all by itself and you can't do it all by yourself.

Extend your planning to your family life as well, supporting your work schedule with meal planning and by asking your family and friends for help when you need it.

Now Take a Deep Breath and Start by Taking One Step at a Time…

Thinking about all that we need to do and be on a daily basis can sometimes feel overwhelming. Give yourself permission to feel a little overwhelmed or afraid, then take a deep breath and start by taking one step forward. Now go and be consistent!

About the Author: Carla is the proud (and totally biased) mother of one very precocious daughter, a loving wife to one very lucky husband, and a supporter of moms everywhere who want to build a lifestyle business that gives them the flexibility to work-from-home and raise a family.

She is a believer that the best business training isn't in the classroom or the boardroom, but the playroom where she hones her business skills on a daily basis. Want marketing help? Try upselling a toddler on carrot sticks instead of cookies. Need to negotiate a contract? Try talking a reluctant preschooler into washing her hair.

She shares her time management, motivation and practical business tips for mom entrepreneurs as well as the trials and tribulations of balancing work, family and a little bit of playtime for mommy at www.MOMeo Magazine.com, an online resource publication for work-at-home moms.

A Satisfying Sunday and a Success Ritual You Can Do In Bed

JENNIFER BOURN

When I began working on my chapter for this book, I did a lot of thinking about what a ritual actually is - a set of fixed actions and sometimes words performed regularly, especially as part of a ceremony.

I spent quite a bit of time reflecting on my daily activities and the things I do on a regular basis that contribute to my success. I thought about attending conferences, listening to teleseminars, hitting the gym, networking, creating "me" time, masterminding, reading, trying new technologies, and more. But they are all obvious actions. I believe that each item listed is an action that I must do to be able to run my business effectively.

I was looking for a ritual, a habit that I created to help me achieve more. I really wanted to share a success ritual with you that is personal and meaningful to me.

Then one morning, I realized that the answer was right in front of me the whole time. I actually have two success rituals that make a big difference in my productivity and my mindset.

The first success ritual I want to share with you is my **Satisfying Sunday Success Ritual.**

Each and every Sunday, when everyone in the house is still asleep, I sneak out of bed and tip toe downstairs. It's still dark, but the sun is just peeking up above the houses and it is so quiet that you can hear the wind whistling and the refrigerator running.

I make a large mug of hot chocolate and sit down at my desk. This is my favorite time of day. No email, no phone calls, no television, no radio, no kids yelling and laughing, no interruptions. There is only me and my thoughts.

In the peaceful silence and solitude of Sunday morning, I clean my desk, file paperwork, condense my scribbled notes into a notebook, replace the magazines I have read with new ones, refill the paper in the printer, clean off the whiteboard, and once again make my office a beautiful place to work.

I am so much more productive and creative in a beautiful work environment!

I spend this time thinking about my own business and my big vision. I think about and brainstorm ideas for marketing, teleclasses, webinars, blog posts, and even products. I think about where I want to go and what I will feel like when I achieve my goals. It is my time to refocus my mindset and recharge my motivation.

Sometimes I get lost in thought. I don't quite know where the time went - maybe to a daydream or a happy memory. It is always a relaxing and invigorating time for me.

Once my office is tidy, I review the achievements of the week prior, identify where each open client project stands, reexamine deadlines, and make a master to-do list for the upcoming week. That way, on Monday morning, I have complete clarity around where I stand and what I need to accomplish.

I also use this time to get a head start on my marketing for the week.

I first look at my marketing calendar to see what the focus of my marketing is for the week. My marketing calendar tells me the topic for my newsletter, what I need to be promoting to my social networks, the theme of my blog posts, and what speaking engagements or events happen that week and in the upcoming weeks, and more.

Before using a marketing calendar, I was coming up with article ideas at the last minute and always worrying about what to post and write about. As a result, I ended up writing about the same things over and over again. But now, I use a marketing calendar and I have all of this information at my fingertips, and I never have to stress over what to write about. I simply use my marketing calendar as an overall guide. This ensures that I am marketing with purpose and that my efforts are moving me closer toward achieving my goals.

Next I write my email newsletter and login to Infusionsoft to schedule it to send during the week. If you aren't yet using an email marketing service provider to send your email newsletter, I highly recommend you look into Infusionsoft, Aweber, 1ShoppingCart, iContact, or ConstantContact right away.

I then write my social networking posts for the week, and login to HootSuite to preschedule posts to LinkedIn, Twitter, my Facebook profile, my Facebook page, and any combination of the above.

If I am feeling really productive, I'll write my blog posts for the week too, login to my WordPress site, format and optimize my posts, and schedule them to publish later in the week. WordPress makes publishing my blog simple, and the Yoast SEO Plugin makes optimizing my content painless.

With my newsletter complete, my social media marketing scheduled, and my blog posts scheduled, I am able to focus more time during the week on my clients without worrying about my own marketing.

My Sunday ritual is extremely satisfying and rejuvenating. It is time I set aside to create a beautiful workspace for myself, review the accomplishments of the past week, plan my workflow for the upcoming week, automate my marketing, work on my business, and just be with my own thoughts. My Sunday morning ritual helps me be more productive, more focused, and more relaxed during the week.

I love my Sunday morning ritual and highly recommend this approach. But I'm a morning person, and I thrive in the early hours of the day. If you aren't a morning person and you'd rather stay snuggled in bed under the covers dreaming away, you can still apply this approach.

You may choose to set aside time Sunday night, or you may choose to set aside smaller amounts of time at the end of each workday to recap the achievements made that day and prepare for the next day.

Whichever approach you choose, just make sure it is quiet time that you have to yourself. Turn off your ringer or forward your calls, turn off the television or radio, close your email, and enjoy the silence.

After all, it is in silence that we truly hear the voices from our heart and soul.

These voices that speak from the depths of our being are a huge part of my second success ritual, a ritual that happens for me when I am still in bed.

When I was in high school, I was a cheerleader and each week we learned new cheers and dance routines to perform at the football and basketball games. Picking up the routines was easy for me – even though I never practiced. Or at least that's what people thought.

It's true. I never physically practiced. But I did practice the routines mentally, going through them over and over in my head. Each time, I pictured myself completing the routine perfectly and thought about the rush I felt when performing in front of a big crowd.

So when it came time to perform, I was ready. I had mentally prepared myself. I knew the routine inside and out and I knew exactly how it felt to hit each move and complete the routine perfectly.

The same principle is applied in my second success ritual, my **Morning Motivation**.

Each night during the week, I set my alarm to go off one hour before I have to get out of bed the next morning. I know it sounds crazy, but even though the alarm goes off, I don't get out of bed. Instead I reset it to off again at the correct time.

For that single hour, I stay in bed, completely relaxed, snuggled tight under the covers with my eyes closed. But I don't go back to sleep. I use that hour to focus my mindset and get ready for a successful, productive, inspiring day.

I think about exactly what I need to accomplish that day and prioritize each task. I think about the projects I am working on, and I visualize myself completing the tasks successfully and checking them off my daily to-do list one by one.

I sometimes design a website in me head, trying different ideas, and moving the design closer to the final. I sometimes write an email I need to send in my head, testing out different things I could say. I sometimes think about a challenge a client is having with their business and brainstorm ideas and solutions.

I also think about meetings or conference calls I have that day and I set clear intentions of how I would like them to go and what results I would like to see from those meetings.

I think about my big vision and where I see myself in the future. I visualize myself as the woman I want to become and my business as the business I am working to create. In this moment, I know exactly how it feels to reach that goal and how it feels to help create change for so many other people.

I also use this time to let my mind wander and dream about new ideas. At this point I am usually still too tired to self-edit or criticize my own ideas. So I let my mind drift and think about all of the what-ifs, the wish-I-coulds, the wouldn't-it-be-nices, and the in-a-perfect-worlds.

Sometimes, one of those thoughts or ideas will crystallize so clearly in my mind that I put the idea on paper that day. Some of those thoughts and ideas get added to my marketing calendar and become a reality for my business.

For that single hour every morning, I lay still in my bed with my eyes shut, completely relaxed and I focus on my mindset.

I think with no distractions.

I wish with no judgments.

I believe with no limits.

This morning ritual helps remind me of why I do what I do, what I am working toward, and what difference I want to make in the world. Each day, I am inspired, motivated, and ready to take action.

The two personal success rituals I shared with you have strong similarities. Both help build a mindset for success, and both are experienced alone and in silence.

Like I said before, it is in silence that we truly hear the voices from our heart and soul, and it is in our mind that we truly see the possibilities that lay before us.

You can't afford to ignore your mindset.

You see, for a long time I ignored mine. I just said yes to the work that came to me, and completed the work because I was good at it. Day in and day out, I did the same thing over and over again. I sent out an estimate, the estimate was approved, the work got done, and the client was billed.

I was pulling down what many would consider a great income, but I was just spinning my wheels. I was in a rut. If I kept doing the same thing, in five years, I would be in exactly the same place.

Whether you have an hour each day, or an hour each week, I urge you to work on your mindset. You may find time driving in your car, practicing yoga, relaxing by the pool, or laying in bed. You may find time during your daily run or a brisk walk, or while enjoying a cup of coffee.

Just make sure that you check in with yourself and reconnect with your inner voices, your hopes, and your dreams in peaceful silence.

Take the time to work on your mindset and nourish it with thoughts of success, love, happiness, and achievement. For when you can clearly see and feel where you're going and what you hope to achieve, the journey getting there and making it a reality becomes much easier.

About the Author: Jennifer Bourn is a custom WordPress theme designer, graphic designer, and owner of Bourn Creative. With more than thirteen years experience in building brands online, she is also the company's Online Marketing Strategist. As creator of the Online Marketing Acceleration System, Jennifer helpssuccessful entrepreneurs elevate their brand, build a website that works, and get found more often online. She is known best for her clean, beautiful,and functional websites, her SEO prowess, and her ability to build a powerful, personal, profitable brand.

Jennifer is also a taco eating, chocolate loving, book reading, television watching mother of two, who spends way too much time at Target and works with her husband, Bourn Creative CEO Brian Bourn. You can find Jennifer online at http://www.BournCreative.com @jenniferbourn on Twitter.

One Size Doesn't EVER Fit All

BETH SHARKEY FLARIDA

Every day I talk to clients struggling with maintaining an organized workspace and increasing their productivity.

They assure me that they have tried over and over again to get organized with no permanent success. They are convinced there are not enough hours in the day to do what they need to do to be more successful.

When I ask why, the response I usually get is this: "I read a couple of books about organizing and tried their suggestions, but they didn't work." "I went to a class and bought all of the recommended things I needed to get organized, but it didn't work." "I've tried all kinds of time management tips but I can't stick with them for very long." You get the idea.

Well, here's the thing: **Productivity and Organization are NOT One Size Fits All! Ever, Ever, Ever.**

The trick is to read hundreds of books, listen to hundreds of speakers and go to all kinds of classes. Learn everything! But that can add to the confusion not the resolution. You really only need to choose the few things that resonate with YOU to shift YOUR problem! That's where I come in. I have studied the methods, the literature and the various presenters for 20+ years. I bring this information to you so that you can quickly get on your way to being organized FOREVER, reducing your feelings of overwhelm and being way more productive than you are now!

It's okay to do what no one else is doing. It's okay to have a system that no one else would stick with. It's your life and your business and it only has to work for YOU! I give you permission to do it your way!

Here we go!

There are several things my clients and I talk about when we begin to work together. Here are some of the questions I ask and topics we discuss. Keep an open mind; there are no wrong answers. All of these things need to be taken into consideration as you create the systems and procedures you will incorporate into your business to be more successful.

Are you right or left handed?

What time of day are you at your best? Are you a morning person? Do you get a surge of energy at 9 o'clock at night? Do you wear out after lunch but get a second wind around 4 PM?

Do you work best when it's completely quiet? Do you need noise in order to concentrate? Does music help you work or do you find yourself singing and dancing around so much that it becomes a distraction?

Are there distractions around your office (or home office)? People? Pets? Children? Traffic noise? Too much visual stimulation? Too many things on the walls? Too many piles on the floor? Is the phone always ringing? Is your email always dinging?

Do you share your office with anyone or are you the only one who works there?

Are you going to have clients visit you in your office?

What items in your office do you use every day? (This could be anything from a pencil to a shredder to a book or a filing cabinet). Make a list.

What items in your office do you rarely use?

What office equipment do you have? (laptop / CPU / monitor / keyboard / mouse / fax / printer(s) / scanner / copier / camera / video / webcam / phones / shredder / other)?

Which of the office equipment do you use on a regular basis? Which do you rarely use?

Which areas of your office are overwhelming for you and feel unorganized? Number them in order of priority. (1 being the most urgent. If a certain area does not apply to you, you don't need to number it).

- Email
- Computer Files
- Computer Desk Top
- Favorites / Bookmarks
- Paper Flow
- Piles
- Your Desk
- Setting Up File Drawers
- Purging File Drawers
- Daily Mail
- Tickler File
- Time Management / Calendar
- Books
- Book Shelves
- Office Space

- Supply Closet / Area
- Other

Describe your business and what you do.

Describe your office space.

What do you do when you're in your office?

What are you not doing in your office that you need to be doing?

What's keeping you from doing it?

What do you feel is your single greatest challenge around getting organized?

What other organizing challenges, obstacles and frustrations are you dealing with in your office?

In a perfect world what would your office look like?

How would it feel to work there?

Now you have a good idea of the information I gather and what goes into the process of getting you together. There are a lot of variables (you, your space and your things) and there is absolutely no way that the answer is the same for everyone. You simply need a plan that's tailored to you and how you want to live and work.

Let's put all of the pieces together.

When you look at your answers and see it all in writing, do you feel overwhelmed? Do you feel relief? Do you feel confused?

Any answer is okay. Here's what I recommend. Start with your space and your things, and then once everything is in its place, work on the procedures and systems and time management.

Considering only your space and your clutter, decide what will give you the most momentum going forward in this project. Would it be getting the most difficult area in your office taken care of or is it easier for you to build momentum by getting one of the 'no brainer' areas of your office done? A difficult area or an easier area? Whichever you choose, begin. It is that simple. Begin.

I want you to take baby steps. Don't try to get the entire office done in a day or even a week. Break the project into manageable chunks. One desk drawer, one shelf, one pile, half a file drawer. Whatever feels doable and not overwhelming.

Another way to chunk the project is by time. Decide how much time you have to devote to this project. Maybe it's 30 minutes a day. Maybe it's 2 hours every Wednesday. Next I want you to set a timer and work only until the timer dings and then come back at the next designated time and work until the timer dings and so on until you are done. You get the idea. What fits for YOU? Breaking the project into areas or time?

Here are some tips to make this as painless as possible.

For purposes of taking you through the process I'm going to assume you are organizing a pile of paper.

Sort through the papers and categorize them into piles that make sense. Use broad categorizies. I suggest 10 to 12 at most. You can always create subcategories later. But in the beginning I want you to choose broad categories so you don't become more overwhelmed by having 72 piles.

As you sort, throw away what is obviously not wanted or needed.

Keep only what you love, need or are legally required to keep.

Very important: As you sort, if you come across a paper you're not sure about, set it aside and come back to it at the end. Don't agonize over it. Put it aside. Sort the papers you can easily decide to keep or toss. Once the easy papers are all sorted then you may go back to the tough ones. I have found the difficult decisions are much easier once you've made so many easy decisions.

It is imperative that once you complete an area or segment of your project, it becomes off limits to piling or messes. There is no bigger momentum killer than having to redo something you already did.

Do not undo or disrespect your hard work. If you must pile until something has a home, pile it somewhere else.

Give yourself boundaries or limits for certain things. We all have certain things we tend to accumulate a lot of. The most common areas I see that tend to overflow and overwhelm are email inboxes, to read piles, file drawers and bookshelves. Decide what level is comfortable and when it turns to overwhelm.

Perhaps you're okay with 100 emails in your inbox? For me it's 12. I don't know why. It just is. And it's okay because it works for me.

You only have so much space for bookshelves and file cabinets. Decide what feels right. Set a limit for yourself. Once you have reached that limit it's time to purge.

For the TO READ pile, I like to use a basket. If it starts to overflow I get rid of the articles I keep passing over in favor of reading something else.

Keep the things you use every day within reach.

Keep the things you rarely use across the room.

The beautiful thing about sorting, creating guidelines, and getting organized is that once you get it together, even when it gets messed up you can quickly clean up and put everything away.

The most important thing I teach my clients is that absolutely everything needs to have a home. The home needs to make sense to you. There should be a reason that you put 'it' there and it should feel right.

Once you get through all of these steps and do the work to get organized you will feel peace. You won't waste time looking for things.

Your things are in their homes and you know where everything is. Your anxiety will be reduced and you will feel a sense of calm.

The next step is to look at the things you listed that need to be done in your office.

You will set up your systems and procedures in much the same way as you set up your space. Decide where it fits, how much time you need and block it out. Group your tasks according to priority, your energy level and deadlines. Remember to break your tasks into manageable chunks.

You also want to plan time to read, file and purge regularly to keep things under control. You can manage your time in the same way you manage your things.

Any time you have something new to put away or need a new system set up you know the process to go through to decide where you should make the home or where to fit it in your schedule.

I really believe that anyone can have success getting organized and being more productive. If you work through the process you can make it all flow. It is simply a matter of not trying to fit a square peg in a round hole.

Once you find your organizing style, it's magic! Find the magic and it's amazing!

About the Author: Beth Sharkey Flarida started her company Get It Together back in 1991. She works with business owners all over the world, as a Productivity Coach, Business Organizer & Efficiency Expert, virtually (online and the phone) and in person. She helps her clients streamline their business activities, structures and systems so they can be more productive, increase their bottom line and reduce stress. Whether it's a minor tweak, major overhaul or a strategic plan, Beth can help you get it together. Visit Beth online at: www.GetBeth.com

Does Success Begin With Being Wrong?

Britt Michaelian

"Every achievement, big or small,

begins in your mind."

— Mary Kay Ash

Several years ago, when I first began my entrepreneurial journey, my goal was simply to be successful. So, I meditated on the word success. I thought about what choices successful people would make if they were in my situation. Honestly, I thought that was pretty much all I had to do to manifest my dreams, just focus on success. And boy, was I ever WRONG!

Very quickly, I learned that in order to be "successful" you have to define what success means to you. Ambiguity gets you NOWHERE in life, which means that focusing on the notion of 'success' is ambiguous and therefore a waste of time.

If you want to live your dreams, you have to know exactly what they are in each area of your life and lay them out with a plan to achieve them. You also have to cultivate a specialized mindset to attract that which you desire. Naturally, this mindset is centered round success, but it is also maintained by clarity and confidence in our vision.

Are you ready to get clear on what you want? If so, why? Knowing the answer to WHY you want to get clear on your goals will be the driving factor behind your success. It is what will pull you through the tough times (we all have them) and it is also what will make the journey worth the while.

Snuggle Up with Your Why

Want to know how to find your why so you can get cozy and fall in love with life?

Simply spend some time with a stack of blank sheets of paper writing out all of the things you want to do and why. Don't filter yourself. Just let it flow. You may get a lot of stuff that seems silly or random, but I guarantee you, the truth will come out eventually and when it does… you will be unstoppable!

Self-discovery of your life mission is not easy work, but one of the untold benefits of getting to know your WHY is that your level of anxiety will decrease substantially. When you have clarity of purpose, you know what to do and why in every moment. This is pretty powerful stuff for women in business. Can you imagine how much more work you could accomplish in less time if you knew exactly what steps you needed to take, when and why to get you to the point where you are living your dreams?

Remember when we were talking about ambiguity? Many people use ambiguity to avoid doing the deep work. They don't reveal what they truly want because they are afraid of failure or afraid of what other people will think of them. However, in the long run when you don't get specific with what you really want out of life, you will find yourself drifting through life, potentially feeling like a victim as life happens to you, rather than feeling empowered as you shape your destiny.

Where Success Rituals Start

I am going to assume that because you are reading this book, you would rather take control of your ultimate level of success than hope that it happens upon you someday. Is that right? If so, then **the beginning of your success ritual needs to start with a commitment to yourself that from this moment forward, you are going to continue to evaluate each step you take for the rest of our life based upon the goals and dreams that you set for yourself.**

The second part of this process has to do with trusting yourself. If you want to know with crystal clarity what your dreams and goals are, you have to be honest with yourself while also trusting that you will discover what your natural gifts, talents and passions are and then honor them by creating a plan to bring them to the world. The level of commitment you have to yourself and to those who need your gifts will determine your ultimate level of success.

Meet Me in St. Tropez

There are times when it may seem very attractive to procrastinate especially if things get complicated or if you are waiting for greater results to be reached. This is why **it is critical that your success ritual involves regularly scheduled vacations.**

When we make it part of our overall plan to include vacations or periods of rest, we honor our own need to relax and rejuvenate while also giving ourselves something to look forward to. So, no matter what kind of vacation you love… cruises, camping, tropical islands, whatever floats your boat… make these part of your success ritual so you can enjoy the ride up.

Your ride up may not be as quick as you think and there is no way of knowing when your tipping point will be, so there may come a time when you are distracted from your main goals. Don't get upset with yourself when you get off track, just dust yourself off and re-connect with your why.

There are two ways to avoid the trap of procrastinating. One is to reward yourself with time off a few times a year. The other is by building a daily ritual designed to keep you focused, inspired and empowered to make your vision a reality.

The Daily Rite

One of the most powerful practices that I can recommend (and that I recommend to all of my clients) is to keep a daily journal that starts in the morning, before your feet hit the floor and finishes just before you close your eyes at night. I have to admit that there are times when I forget to write in my journal and honestly, there is a significant effect on what I accomplish during the day and even on my overall mood. So, I know this practice works!

The reason why this journal is such a powerful tool is because it keeps you laser focused on what is working in your life and business while also reminding you of the gifts that life has already bestowed upon you.

Your success journal can be as simple as a notepad or as tech savvy as an application that allows you to list things on your iPhone. Use a medium that provides the least amount of resistance and has the greatest amount of visibility in your daily life. Whatever medium you choose, make it easy for yourself and start as soon as possible.

This is so easy, it is crazy, but it WORKS with every single person I know who uses this system. So, why not toss your hat into the ring and give it a try? You ready for these simple instructions?

Before you go to bed tonight, place a pen and a pad of paper, your phone or your journal next to your bed. In the morning, before you arise... write down the date, followed by as many things that you can think of that you are grateful for. **Let your gratitude flow.** Don't filter and don't worry about things being silly. Just do it and trust that you are doing it right.

What are you grateful for? The air you breathe, the roof over your head, the clients that love you, the partner in the bed next to you... list them all out. There is no wrong answer as long as you are putting energy into the things in your life that you love and that you want more of.

Next, when you return to bed at night, you will go back to that same page where you listed your "gratitudes" and you will list your successes. What did you do during the day that moved you forward?

Did you make a phone call, send an email, pay a bill, receive a check, drop off the dry cleaning, clear away the clutter, win a contract, sell a book, get a radio interview, give some support, receive a hug or experience some other simple but totally awesome activity? Fantastic! Then, honor it so you can have more! The more you do this, the easier it gets and the more you will see that this is a part of your success ritual that you cannot forget.

We all know that what we focus on grows, so why waste a moment thinking of or talking about anything that doesn't move us in a positive direction?

My success ritual allows me to focus on my dreams while being the person I want to be in this world, doing work that I love and honoring the amazing gifts that life has to offer. Whatever you choose to do as part of your success routine, make sure that it moves you forward in a direction that makes you and those you meet thrilled to be alive each and every day. And there is nothing ambiguous about that!

About the Author: Britt Michaelian, M.A. is a passionate, serial entrepreneur dedicated to helping parents keep their families happy and healthy as they pursue their own personal ambitions. With a Masters in Marriage and Family Therapy and Art Therapy and as the Founder of San Francisco based Responsible Family Company, Britt is well positioned to lead families into a new way of living in abundance.

Join Britt Michaelian as she empowers entrepreneurs to live their life purpose not just by becoming entrepreneurs, but by becoming living, breathing role models for their children.

Visit Britt online at: www.BrittMichaelian.com or @mamabritt on Twitter

Does Waiting for Lady Luck Bring Success?

CATRIONA WELSBY

I am often asked how I manage to squeeze so many things into my busy life. In addition to running the Women's Online Business Academy (WOBA), I also run an online financial services training business. The past few years have certainly brought challenges to my personal life which have directly affected my working life. What surprises people, is how I managed to create my very first online business AND make it a huge success despite an unhappy marriage, making the difficult decision to leave with my young son, coping with a difficult divorce, being a single mom and only working part-time.

Given those difficult circumstances, it would have been very easy for me to run and hide. I did do that for a bit. I loved my son (then 3 years old) and he meant the world to me, but the rest of my life was falling apart. My marriage had failed and I needed to make money fast to support both myself and my family. There were plenty of reasons for me to run and hide rather than take responsibility for my own life, and make the decision to fight for what I wanted and to take action.

So here's my question to you. Do you believe in Lady Luck? Do you believe that the high-achieving female entrepreneurs in this world just 'got lucky'?

I am a huge believer that we all make our own 'luck'. If we sit back, do nothing and let life just happen to us, what kind of 'luck' do you think we will create? On the other hand, if we look at our options, make decisions AND take action, then what kind of 'luck' do you think we'll have then?

Some of the most successful entrepreneurs come from a poor background, and some of the most amazing and inspiring success stories come from them. Some have grown up on council estates, living off handouts from the State and believing that they were destined to a life of hard slog with little reward. For some of them, something has happened in their lives that convinced them that they can achieve whatever they want to achieve, regardless of their circumstances. They haven't simply thought, "This is my lot, I'm going nowhere". They've thought, "I can go out there and be as successful as I want to be, regardless of where I am now". They didn't use their beginnings as an excuse to stand still. I didn't use my difficult personal life as an excuse to stand still in my work life.

I'm an action taker. Sure, I can procrastinate with the best of them, but when a decision is truly important I will make that decision. However, simply making a decision isn't enough. Making a decision to do something doesn't make that something happen. We then have to take action as a result of that decision.

Whenever I make a decision, all people see is a whirlwind. I'm like a tightly coiled spring that has suddenly been freed from its box. I will go all-out to do whatever needs to be done to act on that decision. I identify and work through steps 1, 2 and 3 - I take action.

Here's an example. When I left my husband I suddenly had to make my first online business work, and fast. It was working, but until then I had been re-investing all profits back into the business. But suddenly the money I made from that was all I had, and it wasn't enough to support myself and my young son. I only had myself to rely on to pay all the bills. I could have made the decision to run out and find an employer who would pay me a monthly salary to do a specific job. Instead, I decided that I would do all I had to do to make my business a success. I sat down, did the sums and decided how much I could survive on immediately. But that's wasn't all, I also thought about how much I wanted to be paying myself 6 months down the line. Then I took action. I listed everything I needed to do to bring in more money, and how I was going to do it. My son attended nursery 3 days a week, and in those 3 days, with some evenings thrown in, I worked extremely hard. I did everything I needed to do, and within 6 months the business had grown significantly and I was paying myself a very good salary.

If I hadn't taken action, where would I be now? I imagine I'd be working for an employer, with a completely inflexible work life that my home life had to fit around. I wouldn't be able to go to my son's school plays, I wouldn't be able to take him to school and pick him up every morning. I wouldn't be able to take a vacation whenever I wanted. Instead, I now have a completely flexible work life that fits around my home life, and not the other way round.

Was I simply lucky? Did this success just 'happen' to me? Did I sit down and wait for my dream to happen? No. I created my own 'luck' by making the decision to take control of my life, and then taking action.

After making the decision, it's all about taking action. Without action, you'll still be exactly where you are now in 1 year, 2 years, 5 years, 10 years....

This isn't just true for business, it is also true in our personal and home lives. In October 2010 when myself and my 'Mr Right' (yes, I finally found him!) decided to get married in 3 months time, I just got on with it. Many people looked at me in disbelief wondering how on earth I could arrange a full-blown wedding within just 3 months. Even worse, that 3 months included Christmas and I was also launching a major product for the Women's Online Business Academy (WOBA) and running my financial training business.

How did I do it? I made a list of what needed to be done, and then did everything on that list. Instead of taking weeks or months to come to decisions, myself and my fiancée sat down and made the decisions there and then. The longest we pondered on anything was a week. And the wedding we organised was just as wonderful. Nobody would have known that we had organised everything in just 3 short months. So how did I manage to organise a wedding in only 3 months? By not procrastinating and taking action.

The point is, whether it be in your work or your personal life, if you want something badly enough then you absolutely can go out there and make it happen. Nobody else is going to do it for you, it's up to you. It's your life, live it to the full. Don't spend your last days here on earth wondering about what could have been and regretting what you didn't do. Live your life so that your last days are spent being thankful for what you have achieved, the amount of time you've been able to spend with family and friends, and what a wonderful life you have had.

I continue to take action day in and day out. If I didn't, I'd stand still again and my 'luck' would stop. My businesses would stop growing, my income would fall, my flexible life would slowly disappear, my family's lifestyle would suffer, and my own self-esteem would diminish. So what do you need to do to create your own 'luck'? Here's my 7-step formula.

1. Decide what 'luck' you would like. Write it down. For example, you may want to be earning a 6-figure income from your own business within the next year. Or you may want to only work 24 hours a week but be earning a full-time income.

2. Now write a short paragraph about where you are now. What does your work life look like? What does your home life look like?

3. Now think ahead to this time next year, and write a paragraph about where you want to be then. Not where you think you can get to, but where you actually want to be. This is your destination.

4. This step is extremely important. Make the decision to work towards your destination. Make the decision AND mean it.

5. Think about how you're going to get from where you are now, to your destination. Start by thinking about the first step you need to take. For example, free up some time to work on your goals, arrange some help around the house, research job opportunities. Then think about the next step and the next and the next until you get to your destination. Don't get bogged down in the detail. These steps should be a high level overview. So it's not 'find someone to work for me 6 hours a week on Mondays and Tuesdays doing my washing, ironing and cleaning', but 'outsource domestic tasks'.

6. Put deadlines against each step. Be realistic, but at the same time don't make them too easy to achieve or you'll lack motivation to just get on with it.

7. Take action. Writing down and just looking at your steps will get you nowhere. Take action and carry them out. For each of your steps, divide them into sub-steps so that you have a clear path for achieving each one. By doing this you will work through step 1, then step 2, then step 3.... until you reach your destination.

You are the only person who can make the decision to become a "take action" person. Don't wait around for things to happen to you, make them happen for you. Step up and MAKE the things happen that you want to happen. It's your life, do all you can to live it the way you want to live it.

I don't believe in "Lady Luck" but I do believe that we make our own luck, and a lot of this is down to positive thinking and taking action. Whatever our upbringing, our background and the tragedies that may have happened in our lives, we are ultimately in control of ourselves, our actions and our lives from this point forwards. We can live our lives using our past as an excuse for not achieving our dreams, or we can look to the future and realise that we are masters of our own destiny. It's up to us.

Today is the day for each and every one of us to take control of our lives and create the success we want. Yesterday is part of the past. We all need to learn from our mistakes and experiences and move on, otherwise the rest of our lives will not be the success we dream of. Don't waste another day, make the decision to make a change in your life, and then act on it.

I wish you all the 'luck' in the world. You just need to go out there and grab it firmly with both hands.

About the Author: Catriona Welsby owns and runs two successful online businesses. She set them both up single-handedly, and in the case of her first business this became successful while she also dealt with some extremely challenging personal issues. She is proof that anybody can achieve online success if they make the decision to Just Do It and then Take Action. Catriona is the Founder of the Women's Online Business Academy (WOBA) at www.MyWOBA.com where she shares her knowledge, skills and passion to teach other women who want to achieve the success and flexibility in both work and home life that she has achieved.

It's Time to Get Moxie

CRYSTAL O'CONNOR

I hope this doesn't sound too harsh and maybe you notice it too. But I would like to just say that the majority of us do not take the time to work on our "Moxie." But I am here to tell you, it really does take some Moxie to work up the nerve to get it started, get it going and create the momentum to really reach deep inside of yourself and start to ask those tough questions. Problem is, most of us don't know how to do that. We know we want freedom, so we start without a plan, but we don't bother asking ourselves "why" we are doing it at all…or stop and really listen for the answer of our own inner voice.

If you are anything like me you are guilty! You want it all. I decided this sometime ago. I was definitely plagued with the "want it all" attitude. I also spent far too long talking myself out of that attitude and listening to the voices that led me in their direction.

Trouble was, their direction was not defined. I realize after years of being led astray by the naysayers that their destination was a place called mediocre and was laced with their own doubts, fears and insecurities.

I watched them as they struggled in sales positions, jobs, relationships and other aspects of their life. They did without enough family time, without freedom to travel, with just enough to get by and without getting all they wanted out of life. I watched them lie to themselves and me while they accepted a dead end job they did not enjoy working at and with people they were not inspired by.

And then everything changed when a success ritual of mine turned into what I would call a miracle. However, I did not at the time recognize it as a success ritual it was just something that I decided to take part in.

I included myself in a group of people that intentionally took time out of their week to sit in a small chapel within a larger church. They called it the Perpetual Adoration Chapel. 24 hours a day there was someone sitting in that chapel. So, every week on Thursdays it was my turn, I would show up at 4:00 and sit quietly to pray in solitude. I couldn't reschedule or cancel. I had committed myself to it.

It became a time of solitude that I had never truly let myself experience before. There were no distractions, no voices…just my thoughts. Eventually I began to hear my own voice. It became my time to dream, create and plan. I began to not only hear my voice but to listen as well. I would ask myself a question and the answer would vividly appear in my mind. It was a time of clarity.

A Personal Story

At this particular time in my life I had desired to have a child. For four years there was not a doctor that was able to explain why it not happened for me yet. My investigative efforts had been exhausted by reading every book I could get my hands on about infertility.

One particular day I decided to offer up a white flag of surrender while sitting in the chapel. I decided to make an intentional plea to a higher power or what some may know as the universe. I was very specific with regard to the appearance of a child, any child that needed a Mother and I would be there with open arms.

I left that day with a feeling of relief that I had finally let go of my struggle to become pregnant. It felt like a weight was gone. In my heart I just knew I would be a Mother soon. Exactly three weeks later I received the phone call. My daughter had been born.

That was 10 years ago. My son and youngest daughter were born just 8 and 14 months later. To this day I am convinced that we have a power within ourselves to attract anything and everything we want. It begins with a ritual much like I described.

Quiet reflections in solitude, away from the sounds and distractions of everyday life lead to great abundance and success. It works in all aspects of our endeavors. The trick is to be consistent and to find that place you can call your own. It takes the same commitment it takes for a client or important event.

Taking Stock in Your Internal Assets

What I like to do is to start by asking myself those questions. I'll help you start.

- What is it that your eyes are drawn to in a crowd?
- What is it that pulls on your heart strings?
- What could you do all day…and forget time has passed?
- When you walk into a book store what section are you drawn to like a magnet?
- Can you visualize what it is that makes you stop in your tracks and want more of?

You have an appetite for something. There is something that is called desire in you and you probably think of it daily or often enough that it has become a part of your mental motion picture. In fact, it could be that you think of it so often it has become invisible.

For some it may have become like the landscape that surrounds you and no longer appreciate its value. It is like the door that has blended in with the paint on the wall. You cannot see its handle or its invitation beckoning you toward it. Urging you to open it and peak inside.

Now I want you to think of your mind as being made up of secret compartments. Like a storage compartment made up of a secret cache. If each compartment or cache were to be opened it would display a beautiful arrangement of what we will call YOU. Each cache would spill from it bits and pieces of knowledge, skills, successes and talents. It would also expose your deepest and darkest fears, your weaknesses and your problems.

This was my ritual when starting out in my business. I needed to take stock of my internal assets and liabilities before my ambition could come to fruition. You need to do this too. This is the first ritual to getting MOXIE. Within each and every one of us lies monetized skill or talent.

Moxie really just means to assess and take action. It means you've got experience & talent and the gumption & fortitude to bring it to a place of monetization and profitability. It means you take a look at what you've got, what you want and you begin to get an idea of where you are going and how you are going to get there. Understanding what you want and becoming aware of what is possible leads to confidence and clarity.

IF you were to think of a painter or a carpenter you would understand that they need to assess their tools before they can begin to imagine what they could create with their imagination. So go ahead and begin this first ritual. Begin to write down a list of qualities much like you see below. You have two columns. Make a list of the tools you have to work with.

Experience/Talent

What do you know?

What can you do?

Desire/Passion

What are you good at?

What are your hobbies?

What have you failed at?	What have you learned?
What do you fear?	Whom do you know?
What are your biggest problems?	What do you want?

The bottom line is all talents, skills and desires can be turned into cash. I see too many people spending too much time learning, going to college acquiring several degrees, thinking they need to keep learning before they start cashing in on their knowledge. I say, it's time to start doing and stop being a professional student. I'm all about being a constant learner and believe we never stop learning until the day we die. However, I see people going back to gain yet another degree in another profession or industry. I can't help but think they are avoiding LIFE by doing that.

I mean, life isn't about sitting and learning. It's about learning while doing. I say why not stop and assess what they've got up there in their noggin and start hearing Ka-Ching instead of the other way around.

Okay, now that you get the idea that I'm all about cashing in on your passion, I want to discuss another important ritual I use and I can honestly say it wasn't easy at first but once get the hang of it, it can really be addictive.

Moxie: Verve, action; know-how, pep.

It wasn't until I managed to make an entire mess of my finances that I realized the problem wasn't that there wasn't enough business to capture out there in the universe. The problem was that I wasn't intentionally asking for the sale. I wasn't putting together "profitably directed projects" and taking action. I wasn't taking in all of the opportunities there were. I was leaving money sit on the table as I hovered over it not recognizing it as opportunity. It wasn't until I started seeing the opportunities and setting up systems to attract the buyers did I start really turning my talents, skills and passions into profit. So, what I am saying here is that you have to start using your imagination to come up with products and start offering them up. It's that simple.

I had been in marketing and sales for years in four different industries and never once took my eye off of a goal. For some reason though there was a time that I didn't think that I had to sell anymore once I started my own business. I was FREE! Whoo hoo! Or at least I thought. Then reality sunk in and I realized that the truth is…we will always be selling whether it is our personality, our ideas or our products and services. So, the sooner and better you are able to swallow that jagged little concept the faster you will get to that monetized goal you have in your mind.

Setting up a schedule of activities and committing to them with consistency helps stay on task as well. I make it a habit to take action with my tasks with a year- long laminated wall calendar. I color code it with four segments or tasks. Marketing related tasks are for Mondays, Wednesdays & Fridays, Tuesdays are dedicated to meeting with clients and Thursdays are allocated for catching up with webinars I have specifically set aside, reading and planning the next weeks marketing tasks or projects.

Sticking with a consistent schedule may be the most difficult part of being an entrepreneur I have decided. We want to feel free and do what we want when we want. But the truth is, we have to be consistent with our effort so that we can be free financially in the end. It really is all about setting up your success rituals and sticking to them. Consistency leads to results and results lead to confidence and confidence leads to Moxie.

About the Author: Crystal O'Connor teaches women and children how to start and run profitable businesses while creating multiple streams of income in their life and business. She believes entrepreneurial skills

are essential for building wealth and prosperity as well teaches real-life strategies that help Mothers build empires while raising their families. Crystal began her career in education that quickly led to publishing, sales, advertising, financial products and the real estate industries.

She is the founder of a success magazine called Fearless Ambition and is a speaker, business coach and author of Getting Moxie: A Girls Guide to Money, Marketing and Motherhood. For consulting or to get her free ebook you may find her at www.moxiemompreneur.com; www. fearlessambition.com; www.thekidpreneurclub.com.

Be Happy And Passionate and Watch Your Business Soar!

JANET MAJOULET-FOUST

My adventure into entrepreneurship was not a straight line to success. It had many ups and downs. I remember waking up morning after morning really unhappy about the business I started. I felt like I was getting up every morning to go to a job I dreaded. At first, I couldn't figure out what was wrong. I had started my own business, which was a dream come true, and now I was unhappy? I had to finally take a good hard look at what was going on in my business and with myself.

One day I was on the phone with a very dear friend, and fellow entrepreneur, and I started to spill my heart out to her about how I was feeling and how frustrated I was. I started this business full of hope and excitement. I always wanted to be an entrepreneur, so why am I feeling so upset and disappointed? She listened patiently to me and then sent me on my way with a task, and that was to really think about what I was passionate about in my life and what I really enjoyed doing. Thank goodness for good friends and her support that day. I followed her advice and took it even farther.

First I wrote a list of corporate jobs I held in the past. Then I wrote down the pros and cons of each position. With this process I was able to pull out the positive aspects of the positions I felt really good about. I remembered how I felt so at home in the computer industry that I worked in many years before.

My favorite position in the corporate world was as a technical support manager. I managed two call centers for a large software company and just loved the technical part of computers and software. I also loved helping our customers install software programs and getting the program running correctly on their computers. I was the "go to" gal for all the upset customers too. I was known for being able to calm them down and fix the issues.

The other thing I absolutely loved doing was marketing, which was another position I held for another software company I worked for. Through this process, it finally hit me that what I truly was passionate about was all things technical and that I absolutely loved teaching other small business owners how build and market their business using social media and Internet marketing tools. I took what I learned and decided to get back to my "geek roots"!

I dove in headfirst and taught myself everything there was to know about social media and Internet marketing. When I would learn something new that I thought could be useful, I would test it in my own business. And when what I learned worked, I would write that process down. I could feel that I was on to something big.

During my exploration into social media and the Internet world, I became fascinated with Wordpress, a blogging and website platform, and decided to learn how to customize Wordpress templates and BAM, I was in heaven!

I quickly found through my exploration of all the new things I was learning, was that I was really enjoying the process. I just needed to follow my heart and do what brings me joy and then put that into my business. After I felt comfortable with my processes, I taught others to do the same. This awareness was the start of my business success.

Once I found the joy in my business and was truly happy, I couldn't wait to get back to it when I woke up each day. Everything started to fall into place. I found it so much easier to talk to others about what I did. You know that dreaded question that people ask you; what do you do? It became much easier for me to answer. I was so excited to share what I did, that people I met were much more interested and my perfect clients started to show up without much effort.

Finding my joy in my business was such a big piece to the road to my success that I now coach my clients to go through the same process that I did to find their own happiness and joy in the work that they do. If they feel like they are not on the right path or just not excited about what they are doing, or they don't have clients in their current business, something is not in alignment. Because if you are having fun and are excited about your business, it shows up in everything you do. I find that once they work through their own process, they start to see big changes they get their mojo back and opportunities that they never dreamed of happen. It's magical!

One of the most successful and effective practices I do to keep myself moving forward now is keeping a journal. My method of journaling is to wake up in the morning, when the house is quiet, grab a cup of coffee and sit in my home office and start writing.

My journal, or morning papers as one of my colleague's calls it, is my lifeline. It is time to get focused on my business. It allows me the space to write out all my thoughts, inspirations, and celebrations. It also allows me to work through things that maybe didn't go as planned. The process of journaling allows me to get the big ideas out of my head and onto the pages so that I can easily implement new products and services. It's amazing what I am able to work out during this quite time. I have cooked up the most amazing business plans with this simple practice. It not only helps create my success, it accelerates it.

There are times when I miss a morning or two and I can feel a big difference in my day, almost like a void. So I make an effort to do this daily. There are times that I write for 10 minutes, sometimes 30 minutes, but I don't put a time limit on myself. I know when I'm done writing and it doesn't help me to push past that point. Sometimes when I'm having difficulty writing in my journal and feel stuck, I ask for guidance and the answers just come spilling out onto the pages. The answers are usually right on the money and I feel so much more confident taking the next steps.

There are so many benefits to this practice of journaling for me, but the biggest one is it helps me quickly move from a place of confusion to a place of clarity.

This also works well for my personal life. If my home life is off balance, my business will be too. If I find myself frustrated or upset about something happening at home or with family, I sit and write what I'm feeling at that moment. Once I'm done with my entry in my journal, I find a peace that was not there before, and can more easily deal with the issue I'm facing at that time.

The second thing that helped my business growth was joining a mastermind with likeminded entrepreneurs. Since I am the only member of my family who is an entrepreneur, I don't have much support. It can be difficult at times. When I talk to my family about my business, they either don't understand why I even bother running a business, roll their eyes, or think I should just go find a job and be just like them. So to get the support I need for my big vision, a mastermind works wonders.

I have tried large groups, small groups, unpaid mastermind groups and paid mastermind groups. I feel I do best in a small paid mastermind group with likeminded people who understand entre- preneurship. This usually involves a coach who is leading the group, an accountability partner to keep you focused and on track, and the bonus of new friends. When you join a mastermind group you find strategic partners and joint ventures that accelerate business for all the partners involved. You have so much trust with your mastermind group, business just happens naturally. It also becomes a sacred space for you to share your successes and speak honestly about what isn't working. You will get guidance to work through it at any level.

The ideas that flow from the energy of a mastermind group are unbelievable! You get so many new ideas and learn new concepts that you might not of thought of on your own. The members in your group become your cheerleaders and support system. They give you honest feedback on products or services you are thinking about implementing. If the mastermind group has a good leader, and it should, you will know exactly what to do next and HOW to get to the next step. My tip for you is if you consider joining a paid mas- termind; make sure to pick a group that has a leader who is a couple steps ahead of you in their own business growth. You want to be mentored by someone who has been where you are, and has grown his or her own business consistently.

The third key to my success was to find a solution for the loneliness of working in my home office. They say that entrepre- neurs are the loneliest people in the world, and it sure feels true when you are sitting alone in your office day in and out.

My solution to this problem was to join a couple of the local networking groups. I tried out a couple of groups and found the ones that I felt would benefit my business growth. In these groups, I found like-minded entrepreneurs that have become colleagues. Most of these groups allow the opportunity to speak at their events. This can help you get more exposure and practice your presentation in front of a supportive group. You will most likely do business with each other in this environment as well, which is a great bonus! My tip is to be sure to find networking groups that are not filled with the same type of business you are in. You want a good mix of people who work in different fields so you have a better place to build your business. There are many different networking groups available to you. I recommend eWomen, BNI, NAWBO, or you can find local groups at http://www.meetups.com.

I feel very blessed to have a business that supports my family and allows me the freedom to do things I enjoy. My business has been a great adventure. There are times that I feel like I'm standing on the top of the mountain and other times when I am standing in the valley. Being an entrepreneur has its ups and downs, but I wouldn't want to do it any other way. It's an amazing ride. Remember as you build your business to have supportive friends and colleagues around you to help you on your way. If you really truly love what you do, YOU too can have the business that will create the life you dream of.

About the Author: Janet Majoulet-Foust is social media marketing specialist and website brand designer who helps businesses create their unique brand on-line. Janet also coaches business owners how to use WordPress, Internet marketing and social media to market and monetize their business by creating a brand that stands out from the crowd. Janet has been a featured speaker on many TeleSummit series as well as interviewed by the San Francisco Chronicle and Women's Business Owners News. She is the owner of Two Sister's Marketing, Inc. For a consultation or to receive her free audio interview, you can find her at http://thesocialmediaqueen.com.

Seven Critical Rituals of Online Success to Increase Profits Now

JENNA DREW

Through building my own online business, I have found there are seven important rituals that proved to be the most successful rituals of building a thriving online business.

In a moment, I'm going to share with you these seven rituals that can increase the quality of your life dramatically and be the difference between success and failure of your own online business, but before I share it with you, I need to tell you two important things. Read this closely…

First, the success of your online business is up to you. It is a decision that you commit to yourself and the universe. If you succeed, you are the one responsible.

Second, if your online business fails, you are responsible for that as well.

With any online business, success or failure is your decision.

Whether you know it or not, you are taking a bold step forward by reading this book. You are investing in yourself to grow and learn from some of the biggest and brightest women in online business. It's not enough to simply read through this book cover to cover. You need to take action with these words. Follow the steps that are outlined in this book. Pull your thoughts and ideas into action, and you will achieve your own success.

These are the same seven rituals that have made many of today's internet millionaires. These are the same seven rituals that I have used to build my own internet success story. These seven rituals are so powerful that you can use them to build an abundance of wealth for yourself when you use them correctly.

Here are the seven rituals of online business success:

1. Acknowledge Your Successes

I've always kept a journal, starting from my junior year of college when I studied abroad in France. It's not the traditional "Dear Diary" journal you may have kept in junior high though. I write about my thoughts and feelings, so I can go back to that place and remember exactly how I felt when I re-read my writings.

When I started my online business, I started a new type of journal that I write in every morning. On the cover it boldly states three words – Acknowledge Your Successes. Inside, I do just that.

Starting your own business can be a roller coaster ride, so you need a place to write down all of the good. At the beginning, before I started to make money, I wrote down some pretty silly things like "I found three $75 Google Adwords Coupons" or "I thought of a way to expand my business today." These small successes lead to bigger ones like "I got my first $47 order today" or "I made my first affiliate commission" or "I had my first $2,000 day!"

When you show the universe you are thankful for everything you have, the universe knows you can handle more.

I encourage you to start your own journal today. It does not have to be fancy. Just find a blank notebook at home and write

"Acknowledge Your Successes" on the cover with a black permanent marker.

Then, start writing your first entry. It may feel strange at first, but you'll get into the habit after a few days.

2. Set Appointments with Yourself

When you have an appointment or consultation with a client, are you 100% focused on the task at hand? How often do you give yourself that much focus and attention?

Plan out your schedule and set appointments with yourself. I use Microsoft Outlook to handle my incoming e-mail, and it allows me to easily integrate my calendar and my appointments. Typically, I work at least one to two months ahead of time.

Monday afternoons are my administrative and research days. (Who wants to get up early on Mondays anyway?) Tuesdays are my newsletter publishing days. I know that on Wednesdays I focus on social media and Thursdays I typically work with some of my private coaching clients. Thursdays are by far my most packed days. Friday mornings are article submission days and usually I take the weekend off.

Not a bad schedule right? This is my schedule, it works for me. Over the years, I have learned when my most productive times are, and I know when I am not in the mood to do high-thought provoking activities (Hint: that's why I work on social media on Wednesdays.)

Many Internet Entrepreneurs are afraid of making a schedule because it's too much like a 'real job'. However, I think it is the most productive use of my time, and I know exactly where to go at the start of each day instead of endlessly flailing around in my business.

The beauty here is you are in charge of creating your own schedule, and you only have about a 30 second commute from your bedroom to your home office.

3. Stop Listening to Junk!

If you're anything like me, you're always on the go – running errands, driving to meetings, flying to conventions, etc.

Before I got serious about growing my business, I would spend this time catching up on the latest gossip or listening to music and talk shows. What a waste! Now, I always have a fresh audio book, teleseminar or audio program ready to go in my car or on my iPod.

Whether it takes you a day, week or month to finish the program, you have invested time and resources into making yourself a better person.

At first, I had a hard time listening to audio in the car because I like to take note of the information that strikes of interests or importance to me when I read. However, this is an easy fix. I invested in an inexpensive audio recording device for about $25.

Now, when I come across an important piece of information, I just pull out my recording device and speak. My notes are now a lot more beneficial because my handwritten notes were often quick scribbles of incomplete ideas. (Not to mention, it's a lot safer than trying to write while driving!)

4. Plan, Plan, Plan!

If anyone tells you to skip the planning stage of your online business – run! You can save yourself a lot of time, energy and money when you plan where you want to head in your business.

Your idea is precious, and you must nurture it until it takes on a life of its own. As an entrepreneur, you must walk a fine line while planning your business. If you are too critical during your planning stage, you will extinguish any opportunity for your idea to come to life. If you are too lenient, you will fall for misleading traps or miss profitable opportunities.

As part of my morning routine, I spend 30 to 45 minutes strategically planning my next steps in business. When you spend the time to plan where you want your business to go you become extremely clear about your focus.

With this clarity, it is very easy to spot opportunities that will grow your business and make you more money as well as avoid those pitfalls that are simply a waste of your time.

Your business clarity is what leads you to building an unstoppable brand, and your brand is what will set you apart from your competition.

5. Surround Yourself with People of Influence.

"You are the average of the 5 people you spend the most time with."
– Jim Rohn

There are many meanings of the word mentor. A mentor can be someone you know personally or even someone you've never met before.

When I first started my business, I could not afford to hire a personal coach who was where I wanted to be in life. I got myself a library card, and I checked out dozens of books on individuals who have been successful building their own businesses and fortunes.

As my business progressed, I started to join communities lead by women who inspired me like Ali Brown, Kendall SummerHawk, and Gina Bell. Then, I started attending live conferences, seminars and events held by my mentors.

Through this process, I eventually formed my own mastermind groups that formed the foundation of the International Association of Women Entrepreneurs, a professional association dedicated to the development of female-owned businesses online.

6. Get Help!

One of the fastest ways to create a successful business is to hire help. Today, it is very easy to find a virtual assistant that can help you with everything from marketing to bookkeeping.

The idea of hiring a virtual assistant became very popular when Timothy Ferriss published *The Four Hour Work Week* where he talked about outsourcing his whole business. Ferriss practically outsourced his entire business; however, you don't have to start off that extreme.

My first month in business, I hired a virtual assistant for only one hour a week handling a portion of my marketing. Finding the first task you need to outsource is very easy.

Think about the number one task you dread working on every week and get rid of it!

If you are still at a loss for which task to outsource, then start with administration. Although, admin work may seem like a task you can handle on your own, virtual assistants are very skilled at what they do and will save you endless hours of 'inspirational' work each week. Virtual assistants can accomplish admin tasks that may take you a whole day to complete, leaving you more time to focus on the creative and profit-making ideas.

There are many great resources on outsourcing available. The one I use and recommend is an ebook called Source Control. Visit www.jennadrew.com/resources to find more information.

7. Get in the Kitchen!

No, I don't mean start cooking either. How does a chef know when a meal is done and it's time to move onto the next task? When the timer goes off!

The idea sounds so simple, yet it is so effective. Time management is one of the most important factors in owning a successful business.

Do you ever lose track of time checking emails, updating twitter or commenting on blogs? Although it may seem like only five or ten minutes wasted, your time adds up. By the end of the week, 15 or 20 minutes here or there could turn into hours lost!

Do yourself a favor and get a timer. Set it for each task throughout the day and when the timer goes off – move onto your next task. This will keep you focused on accomplishing the task at hand giving you another success to acknowledge in your success journal.

I want to end with a word of advice for those of you brand new to the opportunities of building an online business. There is a reason you are reading this book, whether you're just exploring the thought of entrepreneurship or you are ready to take your first step.

There are four necessary steps to creating a thriving business:

1. Find a need currently not being met.

2. Research and understand your customers.

3. Fill the need in a way that will connect with your customers.

4. Provide superior value to keep your customers coming back for more.

Life constantly changes, so does business. Stay current on industry trends and open to developing new ideas. As your experience grows, you will be able to recognize your most profitable ideas through intuition.

Until then, take your first step towards financial freedom. What are you waiting for? Get out there and start building your own lasting legacy.

About the Author: *Jenna Drew is the author of Legacy Building: The Ultimate Guide on How to Build a Successful Online Business and Create a Lasting Legacy, one of today's best-selling ebooks on starting a successful online business to help you build your own legacy. For 20 free videos covering the top questions asked about starting an online business, visit www.SavvyAndStrongWithJenna.com. If you'd like to network with hundreds of other women entrepreneurs online who are currently making life-changing income, visit www.IAWEO.com.*

Quantum Leaps in Life and in Business through the Power of Conscious Creation

JENNIFER LONGMORE

Have you ever wondered why some women grow in leaps and bounds (and make it look easy)? What about the women who are oozing potential which everyone can see but themselves?

I did too and that is why I studied successful women so that I could observe what the "secret" formula was. Then I applied some of these formulas when I launched my own healing business several years ago, and to my delight, I achieved my five year goals in just three months, which included reaching 6 figures in my first 10months !

So how did I do it?

To begin, I needed to choose success over fear. As long as I gave fear the power to stand between me and my dreams, I knew that I would still be in the same frustrating place several years later. Once I realized this, the choice became easy and I felt very empowered. It was in this moment that I *really* realized that everything is a choice.

Personal responsibility is a fundamental ingredient for conscious co-creation and for achieving success in quantum leaps.

The next step that I needed to take was commitment to my vision and my goals. Without a solid commitment to anything, the energy behind it is just wishy-washy and it goes nowhere. I have experienced this myself and witnesses it in the thousands of women that I have coached over the years. Another way of looking at this is that indecision *is* a decision. Making a decision and then committing to it is essential for forward movement and goal achievement.

Commitment is the rocket fuel to any successful endeavour.

Once I committed, and kicked fear to the curb, it became very clear to me that I needed to approach all opportunities with awe and wonder. This meant I couldn't play small, worry about rejection, or settle for less than I what was aligned to my vision. I knew that I needed to stay in a mindset of being curious, exploring and not being attached to the outcome.

For example, in the beginning of my business, I chose to be open to all ideal opportunities (and I wrote out that list so that I could be clear on what was a good match for me). Then I adopted the mindset of openness and non-attachment as I approached various venues to speak, colleagues to partner with, potential clients to coach, and so on.

I imagined that I was walking up to a series of doors of opportunity that were presented in front of me. With each door that I approached, I tried the door handle, and if it opened easily, I walked through it to determine if I wanted what was on the other side. Alternately, if it was a struggle to turn the handle or if the door was clearly padlocked and never going to open, I was thankful since I didn't needed to spend unnecessary time and energy trying to open a door of opportunity that didn't glide open.

The doors of opportunity that I loved the most were the ones that I barely needed to tap on and they flew open with a warm welcome. Once I found those doors, I committed to only walking through those thresholds from that moment forward. This has been a huge key to my success; that is, allowing energy to flow and only moving towards opportunities that took very little forcing on my part.

The doors of opportunity fly open with welcome arms when we partner with the universe as a conscious co-creator to make our vision come alive.

So, choosing a mindset of success, commitment, and wonder, while partnered with the deep knowingness that I always create my own reality has allowed me to make continued quantum leaps in my business (and my life) ever since.

An integral part of these quantum leaps has been creating regular space for conscious co-creation rituals or practices.

Ever since I blew the lid off of my 5 year business goals in three months when I first launched, I have been using the following practices to stay in the flow and to continue experiencing the immense joy that comes from inner transformation that success instills.

There are several practices that I have which span my physical, emotional, mental, and spiritual aspects which I would like to share with you. I have broken them into categories in the hopes that one from each area may resonate with you that you can implement right away to accelerate success in your life too.

Conscious Co-creation and My Physical Body

I have learned over the years that it is essential to manage my energy by determining who and what gets into my energy field. I have declared that my body and my energy are NOT toxic waste dumps.

What does this mean?

I do not allow low vibration, processed or dead foods into my body. I have been raw vegan for some time and I don't smoke or drink. This is not for everyone, and I certainly do not judge people who choose otherwise. I simply monitored how I felt and when I was at my optimum, and concluded that it was this lifestyle. When you really tune into your body and what it needs, you'll discover your own lifestyle as well (if you haven't already).

Since I do not allow toxins into my body, I most certainly do not allow toxic people in either. I enjoy surrounding myself with success-minded, positive people who are choosing to make a difference on various levels.

It is said that we are a reflection of the five closest people that we surround ourselves with.

I know this can be a touchy area for a lot of women, since we're really good at playing nice and listening to people's problems, but believe me, it doesn't serve. In fact, it doesn't serve either of you. If there are people that you don't feel ready to let go of or family members that you feel you must see even if they bring you down, simply asking to change the subject (and offering up the topic) or sharing that you don't feel comfortable discussing (_____) can often be enough.

I know this may sting a bit, but being the martyr is not a trait of successful people.

Aside from being clear what enters my body, I also gift myself the time and space at the beginning of each day for physical exercise. It truly is an invigorating way to start my day and sets the tone for everything that unfolds. I block this off in my calendar just like any other appointment so that I honour the commitment. I also gift myself weekly body treatments such as massage, acupuncture, reflexology, facials or pedicures.

A common experience for many helpers, is to suffer from caregiver-fatigue. Since I spend much of my week caring for others, I know how important it is to have someone care for me (even just an hour refuels) so that I am always at my optimum for myself and my clients. I highly recommend that you find a way to build this into your success rituals.

I would also be remiss if I didn't mention going to bed earlier than planned so that I can actually fall asleep for seven hours. So often, I witness women making sleep their last priority when it really should be their first. When I don't get enough sleep, I'm moodier (which is not how I choose to show up for others), I am far less creative, my problem-solving abilities are not up to par, and I overlook details (sometimes critical ones). Since I have chosen to be a conscious co-creator in all that I do, I know that sleep is when I integrate and receive inspired ideas for the next day. I also know that I choose to be at my optimum because it serves everyone, including me.

If this feels tricky for you right now, start small and add another 15 minutes to the sleep you're getting now, then 30minutes, then 45, until it seems easy to just gift yourself another hour.

Conscious Co-creation and My Emotional State

Before I leave my bed each morning, I have a conversation with Spirit about how I want my day to unfold, which includes my mood, my energy level, what I choose to attract, how I would like certain events or conversations to unfold and whatever else I may wish to add into the conversation. Connecting in like this on a daily basis is a huge part of being a conscious co-creator and it determines how my emotions will be throughout the day since I am choosing how I intend to show up.

As I move through my day, I experience that which I have chosen. If I experience something that is triggering an emotion, I choose whether I want to participate or if I want to reframe my experience. It is a process, and one that becomes easier over time.

I believe it is essential to pay attention to emotions because it signifies to me that something needs to change. For example, when

I become irritated by something in my business, it means that either something needs to be released, delegated or a system created. Once this occurs, flow is restored *and* there is room for new to come in, which is often more success and flow.

The great thing about emotion is that it is a sign that an aspect of us is ready for a quantum leap.

In fact, what I have found for myself, and what I have observed with other successful women, is that the greatest growth occurs when things are released. Sometimes this is people, sometimes this is stagnant emotion, old mindsets, old systems and so on, but something always has to go. More importantly, when we are being called to release something, we are usually about to make a quantum leap.

My coach's recommendation to you is to pay close attention to the emotions that you experience throughout your day, acknowledge them, trust that there is something better waiting on the other side, and celebrate them as your first sign to a quantum leap that you are about to make. Then give yourself permission to change and witness what shows up for you.

Conscious Co-creation and My Mind

Have you noticed that your ego mind does a really good job at trying to convince you that you can't have it all?

I like to give ego an "E" for "effort"! It really does try, but it wil never get an "A+" from me! Part of being a conscious co-creator is challenging the inner critic and choosing your desired mindset which will shape all of your experiences.

Aside from beginning each day in conversation with Spirit, I also like to read something inspirational to jump start my thoughts into high gear. I keep a book of inspiring quotes by my computer that I refer to each day and I take a midday break to listen to an inspiring teleseminar or audio book so that I maintain my co-creative mindset throughout the day.

I also have mindset questions that I ask throughout the day when I want to show up a certain way to an event, with a client, or just in general. These are particularly helpful when I am posed with a sticky situation or unchartered territory, and they have helped me (and my clients) attract amazing opportunities, huge leaps in income, and many other miracles.

For example, I ask questions like, "what would a seven figure business owner do in this situation?" Or, "how would a spiritual leader respond to this client?" Or even, "what would a stellar friend do in this instance?"

You can imagine how this can instantly shift me into the mindset that I choose to be operating from, particularly as a conscious co-creator.

To take this further and to use a business example (of course, this can be applied to any situation), I have learned that is very important to be intentional before a large networking event. So, I may intend something like, "I choose to be a social rockstar and to be an attraction magnet for an abundance of ideal opportunities, collaborations, and clients." Then throughout the event, if I don't feel like this is happening, I can ask myself something like, "what would a social rockstar do in this situation" or "how would a highly sought-after entrepreneur act at this event?"

Success is almost 100% mindset and then action. Without an aligned mindset, attaining success will feel like trying to push through molasses.

To that end, intention setting has always been a regular part of my success rituals and I block this off every quarter for review and revamp.

I have created a 5 year vision which is the ideal of where I would like to be in all areas of my life. Just doing this sets things into motion. Then I review this at least once a year and break it down into doable action steps for the year that will bring me that much closer to my vision.

For example, I create intentions for the year based on who I want to become, what I want to learn, what I want to experience and what I want to achieve. I typically list 3-5 items in each category. Then I review them every quarter to see what has been achieved and what still resonates.

I have used this method for years and it accelerates my goals each and every time. I highly recommend that you try it and witness what you create.

Here's another tip: I also choose at least three items from my "bucket list" to put into one of these categories that I feel are a stretch but still doable. This keeps me moving forward and avoiding the infamous "rut."

There is a saying amongst successful people, which is "learn to become comfortable with the uncomfortable." As a conscious co-creator, I choose to embrace discomfort with excitement because I know that a quantum leap is just around the corner!

Conscious Co-creation and My Spiritual Connection

Aside from some of the spiritual practices that I already shared throughout this chapter, there are several other practices that I engage to ensure that I balance human doing from human being. The best way that I know how to do this is by returning my awareness to the present moment.

I have regular breathing breaks throughout the day since breathe is our first awareness of being alive and being present. I also use time prompts, so if I look at the clock and it's 10:10, 11:11, 12:12, 1:11,

2:22, 3:33, 4:44, or 5:55, I smile at the synchronocity and I take a moment to pause and breathe, and really connect to the awareness that I am more than what is occurring in that moment.

I also build in regular mindfulness practice, such as meditation or yoga, so that I can bring my attention into the present *and* make myself available to receive inspired ideas through this connection. I highly recommend a practice that feels right to you. This is such an essential component for most (if not all) successful entrepreneurs, especially those that are part of the new wave of conscious business.

Each Sunday, I block off time for spiritual connection and read spiritual material that reminds me of the bigger picture and my bigger role on the planet so that I can stay connected with what really matters. Do you have a regular spiritual practice? If not, even just a few hours per week or 15minutes a day is enough to get stared.

Most importantly, I hire a mentor because if I don't invest in my growth then who else will? Not only do I have a coach for business, I also have one for my spirit and my mind. We all need a cheerleader who can remind us of our greatness, of our infinite potential and of our divine gifts and purpose. This is, by far, the golden key to success and I highly recommend that you get clear on what you need and who is an ideal match for you so that you can receive the support you need to move forward with your life and your vision.

The golden key for all successful people is support.

Now is your time to shine, to radiate your brilliance and to share your gifts in an even bigger way. If not now, then when? There is never going to be more time in the day, or the right time; the time is now! What small step from this chapter can you implement right away to accelerate your journey of success? Kick fear to the curb, commit to your dream, restore your child-like sense of wonder and, as Michael Jordan says, "just do it!"

About the Author: Jennifer Longmore, North America's Soul Purpose Expert, is an internationally acclaimed radio host, healer, teacher and founder of Soul Journeys® School for Spiritual Studies. Not only is she highly sought after for her instant success strategies in creating profitable, sustainable healing businesses, but also for her remarkable intuitive abilities.

For more than 15 years, she has awakened thousands of clients, just like you, to their soul purpose, through high-level private sessions, group coaching programs and certification classes so that they can live their most abundant, joyous path.

Ready to breakthrough to the next level of your soul's journey? Visit www.souljourneys.ca and receive your Soul Acceleration System today!

Defining Success and Understanding Me

JENNIFER UREZZIO

A couple of years ago, I created the *Soul Language Blueprint for Success*. The whole blueprint is based on your greatest desire. In developing the tool and really understanding who I was, I realized that my greatest desire was – success.

I also became conscious that I define success as a result. So at that time in my life, I wasn't feeling really successful because I "didn't seem to be getting any results." I was in struggle. My greatest desire was to be successful and I didn't know HOW to achieve it.

I took classes, I studied the way others "did success" and I talked to peers. What I "forgot" to do was really spend some time with the one individual that had all the answers to creating my own success – ME. I mean truly spend time with me -- not the "fast food" version of time I gave myself because I was focused on everyone else but me. The greatest turn-around in my business was when I decided that I WAS of value and took care of me. On a practical level, this meant not working until 11:00 p.m. each night to get out that last email to a prospective client. On a spiritual level, this meant feeling my own value each day in every fiber of my being -- feeling that I was loved and supported and that there was always a solution.

The truth is that I can share those tips with individuals. I can ask individuals really good questions that can jump start the conversation between them and their Soul. I can even tell an individual, as an intuitive, what I see for them but in the end it is up to each individual to define and be the success they desire.

Here are some of the steps that I took to live and be the success I desire.

Step I – Define What Success Is

- It's your life, it's your success -- This is your chance to really craft what success is and let go of other people's definitions.

- The Feel of Success -- Remember that the most important aspect of success is how you feel, not what you have. How will you feel writing that best seller or landing that big client?

- Write it in stone -- Write this definition and vision down.

Step II – Create a Success/Gratitude Journal

- Savor the success -- If one of your core misbeliefs is that you are not enough, you will gloss over your successes. Each day, write down in your journal your success (even if you feel they are tiny) and as you do, take the time to show yourself, the Divine and the Universe gratitude.

- Focus on you morning and night -- I suggest setting aside five minutes in the morning or your daily intention (see below) and then five minutes at night for your success/gratitude. I fought journaling for years and then I stuck with it for more than a week and it transformed my life. My journal is a place where I spend time with me, just being me. There's no role playing, no facades and no judgment. It allows me to express the profound love I have for the Divine and myself and also allows me the opportunity to argue, scream and rant if I need to.

Step III – Set Your Yearly, Monthly and Daily Intention

- Yearly intention -- Utilize this intention as your "target" for the year. Each product, each client and each choice you make needs to be aligned with this intention. If it isn't, you get to course correct or let something go.

- Monthly intention -- This is where you get to check in with your Soul and request resources that will fulfill your yearly intention.

- Daily intention -- This is where you get to show the Universe that you can live in the moment with joy and happiness.

- Focus on the controllable goals -- Often we focus on unattainable goals like: "I want 82 people to sign up for…" Create goals that you are in control of such as: "I am creating a program that I'm passionate about, love to share with individuals and give people the opportunity to be empowered. The program is filled with ideal clients, who pay and respect me."

Step IV – Asking and Receiving

- It's o.k. to ask for the business -- Often we assume that our prospective clients, family and friends and even the Universe know what we want, desire and need. Guess what? They don't! Asking is so important. Many a time, I have heard from an individual, "Oh, I didn't know you needed or wanted that." Here's the key to asking: no attachment. You need to know that no matter what you are being loved, supported and provided for.

- Learn how to receive -- Individuals who are strong and courageous often have trouble receiving. If success comes knocking at your door you have to be willing to open it. Receiving is you opening the door to success. I suggest that you connect with your Soul and hear from the Divine why it is your right to receive and by doing so you help your community and the world.

Step V – Letting Go

- The rest isn't up to you -- Often we try to control everything in our lives to ensure that things will happen just the way we would like them to...success is about letting go. So the question I ask clients is: "What do you get to let go of to be and live your success?" I suggest that individuals ask this question daily because that answer will change.

Last Step – Do It Again

- There is no end to the journey -- The good news is that your journey is never-ending, the bad news is that your journey is never-ending. It's all about your perception. There is no limit to success, just like there is no limit to joy or love. Once you rise to the level of success that is in your yearly vision, the next year brings a new vision.

There are some things that I believe everyone should know as they create the life that they desire. Some of these I learned the hard way with lots of practice, financial lost and struggle. It doesn't have to be that way. Success doesn't always have to be work and it doesn't have to be hard. It is your perspective.

Tools to change your perspective from fear and doubt to success:

- **Fear is like that plant from "Little Shop of Horrors":** The more you feed it the bigger it becomes. When you are in the midst of fear, this is your indication to do something different. A couple of options are dance, laugh, journal, sing, re-read your success journal, etc.

- **Dr. Seuss was rejected a 101 times:** The world would be a different place if we didn't have the words of Dr. Seuss and yet he experienced 101 rejections. Don't stop trying and believing. A rejection is the chance for you to check in with your Soul and ask what belief you get to let go that isn't serving you. Remember, a failure just means that you haven't asked the Universe for enough.

- **Don't let the past be your future:** Often we let past experiences shape our future. I always ask clients these questions: what did you learn from the experience and how can you apply that to this situation in love and harmony for yourself. You will be amazed at what happens.

The one item that I want individuals to take away from my experiences is that success is personal and you can create that personal experience any way you want. Utilize tools that work with your mind, body and spirit and turn to the true resource -- your Soul.

About the Author: Jennifer Urezzio is a master intuitive, author, teacher and speaker. She founded her own business, Blooming Grove, Know Soul's Language's parent company, in 2004 in response to her intuitive senses and ability to help others feel better about themselves both holistically

and naturally, working closely with them to generate a feeling of strength and well-being.

She also founded a new paradigm of divine guidance — Know Soul's Language — where she guides clients to understand their Soul's Language. This new way of understanding how the soul expresses itself is being embraced by top healers, lifestyle coaches and CEOs all over the country. www.KnowSoulsLanguage.net

Client Attraction and Retention Rituals

KATRINA SAWA

How to build a list of loyal followers who want to know what you're doing and who want what you've got.

I've always been a very outgoing, inspiring and tell-it-like-it-is type of gal; growing up, in college, with dating, in my jobs in the past and now in my own business.

My expertise lies in the traditional advertising, sales and marketing world. I love talking with anyone about anything and I now realize that is such a huge gift that many people are not blessed with. It makes it so much easier to 'sell myself' so to speak in my business whereas many women have such a hard time with this.

When I started my business in 2002, I didn't utilize the Internet very much. I had a website and an email newsletter but I had no idea what else was possible for me online.

I was a networking fanatic. I attended an average of fourteen business networking events every month, meeting hundreds of new people; this is what built my business. Without my consistent and persistent type of follow up, there was no way I'd be where I am today with a multiple six figure business.

One of my main success rituals has always been how to constantly and effectively meet as many people as possible in order to build strong personal relationships with them and then entice them to want my services or products.

In the last year or so have I come up with a simple three-step system for doing this that I've been teaching and implementing all these years but never put into a system.

This book is the first place I am sharing it and this information can dramatically change your life and increase your business' success just like it did mine!

Can YOU Do This Too?

Let me clarify that what I'm about to share with you is not just for those of you who are outgoing or like sales and marketing. The way I teach this can be easy for introverts and less-savvy or salesy entrepreneurs as well.

What Do You Have to Do?

My three-step Client Attraction and Retention System is simple, let me share it with you and then I'll explain each step more in depth.

1. You have to get in front of more people, more often and in more ways

2. You need to make it easy for people to buy from you

3. You need to develop and consistently implement an interactive, relationship-oriented follow up system

So this may seem too simple, but I'm telling you, hardly any entrepreneur I know does this very well, if at all.

This is where most entrepreneurs get stuck and then don't implement.

Step #1: Get in Front of More People, More Often and in More Ways

With the Internet these days you could literally get in front of thousands of people every week, but are you?

In the traditional marketing world they used to say 'it's a numbers game'. In fact in a job I had years ago selling stuff door to door we used to have a goal to knock on 100 doors every day in order to make 10 sales and it worked.

How many people or prospects do you typically need to talk with or come in contact with in order to get 1 client, or 10 clients? This is the first thing you want to consider.

Then, where are your prospects? Are they online, offline, at seminars, at home, in business? Where do they hang out and what are their interests?

You want to find them, groups of them preferably, and then interact with them consistently.

One of the easiest ways to do this is with social networking. You can literally connect with thousands of potential prospects every day if you know where to go, what to say to them when you find them and how to get them to interact with you.

Obviously you can become their friend, comment on their walls, send them messages and I say do all of that. But there is more to it than that.

For example, if I see someone who looks like they may have just started their business, I might take a moment and click over to look at their website. Then I would ask them how their website is working for them (knowing by looking at most new sites, sometimes self-built, that they probably aren't contributing at all to their success) or what kind of challenges are they running into?

They typically respond that it's not really working plus usually they expand on that and tell me numerous other challenges they seem to be having getting started and attracting clients.

I then respond with some suggestions about their site and other things they can do all while encouraging them to contact me for a complimentary Business Strategy Session.

Not everyone I try to connect with online responds to me; in fact a very small percentage of them do but these are the hot prospects. Then out of those people whom I personally interact with about their business or challenges, a certain percentage actually take me up on my offer for a complimentary session.

See how I've made good use of my time here? I don't talk with everyone whom I meet; only those who 'raise their hands' and want help.

The thing I didn't mention about those initial contacts I make is that I don't even do that myself anymore. I started doing it myself but quickly learned the percentages of those who would respond and I also discovered that I could literally write the same message to anyone and the percentages would be the same.

I developed a template of what to say initially to connect on social sites and online forums and now one of my assistants does that for me, saving me hours and hours of my time. Therefore, my time is spent only talking with hot prospects whereas my closing ratio tends to be much higher as well and my time is well spent.

In addition to the social networking sites, you can also get in front of more people with the following strategies:

- Holding your own free event, live workshop, teleclass, podcast or webcast and then marketing it to your list and the masses to build your list.

- Being a guest expert on someone else's teleclass, radio show or live event; getting in front of their audience gives you access to a whole new group.

- Running your own radio show. It's pretty easy to get an online radio show and before you know it you could have a ton of followers.

- Start running video tips on your blog or YouTube, write a blog and market that, get subscribers and then market other things to them as well.

- Do more in person networking. There are always events and seminars you can attend, locally or nationally depending on your target market and reach.

Step #2: Make it Easy for People to Buy From You

The key with this step is to automate as much as you can and also prepare as much as you can, let me explain.

Making it easier for people to buy online or on your website means to have the right functionality and systems on your website, blog and everywhere you exist online.

You want to provide opt in boxes, subscribe now buttons, offers to get free stuff and then click to buy buttons and shopping cart on your website.

95% of the businesses that I see every month can do this regardless of what you're selling.

This means though that you definitely do not build your website yourself, you want to get a professional to help you.

You may not know what you need to know to tell that web designer and they may not know what to ask you either in regards to better sales or conversions online so be careful.

You do want to seek a professional business or marketing coach to help you figure out your big picture plan with your online and of-fline marketing because all of it has to flow together and be easy for the prospect to navigate and buy.

If you aren't sure what an opt in box is or why having a shopping cart or any of this would help your business be more successful, you seriously want to go get my freebies on my website and start learning what else is possible for you.

In addition to making it easier online, you want to make it easier offline for people to buy too.

For example, for most businesses you can sell your products and services when you meet someone in person right?

Why not bring order forms and take credit cards when you go out networking?

I do this every single time I attend a networking function and about eight times out of ten I end up getting a new client.

But what happens if you wait and call them up later or send them an email to your website later to buy later? Typically nothing; I'd say one out of ten might become a customer when you don't make it easy for them to buy.

Step #3: Develop and Consistently Implement an Interactive, Relationship-Oriented Follow Up System

This is the easiest step. Once you develop a system that you like and that works to bring in prospects and retain customers then you can delegate pretty much all of it and you don't have to do any of it.

The problem is most entrepreneurs simply dislike doing follow up. Most of you really have no idea what to do or what to say or you feel pushy when you do follow up so you choose not do it, right?

If not, great then you're probably in the one percent of entrepreneurs who actually do a good job at your follow up.

You want to start by developing templates.

Remember when I said prior that I realized I could say the same thing to each person online whom I was introducing myself to and I found the same results?

Well, it's the same with your follow up. You want to develop the right series of messages that will inspire, entice or encourage your prospects to interact with you, take action with you, buy from you or at the very least find out more information about what you do.

There are all levels of prospects; those who are ready now for what you have to offer, those who've thought about it but are in research mode and those who need it but it's not even on their radar yet or it's starting to become an interest or need.

Your messages should come in as many forms as possible. You can't just send an email newsletter anymore for example and don't get me started on why you shouldn't add everyone to your email newsletter that you meet; that's just wrong!

You want to send an email newsletter but you also want to send something in the mail (hardly anyone does anymore which is why you want to do this – you'll stand out more than ever!). You want to make personal phone calls, you may want to find them on your social networking sites and friend them and if they're local you could even stop by their place of business if they have one.

Each of these ways to follow up could require a slightly different message or call to action.

When calling someone to follow up for example, it might be best to try to build a personal relationship while also reminding them to look out for an email from you or to find you on Facebook.

When emailing to follow up you don't want to immediately just add someone to a newsletter for example, you will get better results, more interaction and less unsubscribers if you first send them a simple follow up note reminding them where they met you, who you are and what you talked about.

You can still send that initial email message to multiple people if you phrase it right. See how a template can be developed after you go out networking or meet someone at an event?

So, developing your system includes writing template emails, online messages, phone scripts possibly and even pre-printed postcards or something you can easily slip in the mail after a meeting.

Then the implementing of your follow up system requires consistency. You can't just send one piece of mail or make one phone call or send one email, you need to do so much more than that.

You want to have a schedule of what emails will go out when, which mailers will go out and when, and when to check in by phone or social site for maximum exposure and response.

About ten years ago, it used to be that you wanted to follow up with a prospect with about seven touches and now it's more like twenty-eight in the course of the first couple months.

Twenty-eight touches isn't really that many however. It could be one initial email follow up message, a few email newsletters, couple phone calls, 2-3 direct mail pieces, four tweets and a dozen social media messages or comments.

You want to do whatever is going to keep you and your products and services on top of mind at all times with your prospects and everyone you meet because you never know when they or someone they know will be in need of what you offer.

How to Get Started Yourself

I mentioned delegating throughout these three steps and I firmly believe that most entrepreneurs will not create a successful six-figure business without a support team.

In my opinion you need to be doing everything I've mentioned in this chapter and more but you definitely should figure out a way for much of it to get done without you having to do it; whether that means getting one assistant or five.

All of this should be in your business and marketing big picture plan. If it is not currently, you want to do everything in your power to change and implement these strategies. These are some of the least expensive and most effective marketing and business practices that I've seen and used myself as a home-based entrepreneur.

I never thought I would have clients all over the world doing coaching sessions over the phone or holding group training programs for entrepreneurs who want to live a bigger, more fulfilled and happy life.

I didn't know what I didn't know back then but the difference was that I kept my eyes and ears open to all kinds of new ideas. When I learn of people doing things differently, running their business in an easier manner; I make decisions to change things.

I took a huge leap of faith because I knew I was worth it, destined for bigger things and to help hundreds of thousands of women entrepreneurs. I had to step out in faith, there was no plan B, no turning back.

You can do this too, I know it. If you're passionate about what you're doing, you can do anything you want, even sell yourself.

I encourage you to take leaps of faith for yourself now; it can be a baby step or a giant leap but if you don't do it now I'd bet you won't do it ever.

About the Author: Katrina Sawa is known as The JumpStart Your Biz Coach and she coaches women entrepreneurs around the country how to work smarter, not harder at developing their own passionate and

profitable business. She's been featured on the Oprah and Friends Radio Network as well as a few news stations in her local Sacramento, CA area. Katrina has a bi-weekly radio show, weekly video tips on YouTube and she speaks all over the U.S. at women's business conferences and seminars.

If you're ready to learn how to build a profitable business that you're passionate about working the way you want to work schedule a complimentary Big Picture Business Strategy Session. Find out how to apply on Kat's private free gift page. You'll get a few free gifts too. www. JumpStartYourMarketing.com/gifts.

No Time, No Money, No Excuses: How to Create Part-Time Success (In the Real World)

KIM PAGE GLUCKIE

In order to truly be helpful to the slowly rising stars who are part-time small business owners, this chapter is designed as one part butt-kicking, on part cautionary tale and many parts inspiration and information. If you are a part-time entrepreneur, or planning to be, you must proceed knowing you have less time and less money to make mistakes, that you must have more passion and conviction to grow your business in the battle against the demands of daily life, and that you must know what success really looks like for you. If you can adopt a "no time, no money, no excuses" attitude, then you can succeed!

In the beginning I mostly knew what I was getting into. My entrepreneurial spirit was part of me through my traditional marketing career working for very small technology companies. I had the bug early on, admiring the rollercoasters of successes and failures and learning the fortitude required to follow through on passionate ideas.

My specific solo-journey began like many (even if you won't admit it) by dipping my toes into direct selling waters. My venture in selling children's books through home parties was a really a delightfully addictive hobby designed to avoid returning to corporate life. And one that opened my eyes to a world of incredibly amazing women – millions of North American women – starting all kinds of small businesses, direct selling businesses, entrepreneurial ideas in an eagerness to feel whole, make a difference, take care of their children while earning some money for necessities and luxuries. Most of these women were like me, needing to make an income but trying to figure out how to do it without being caught up on their traditional careers anymore, or as much.

But unlike me, all these women were struggling to find great marketing advice and were making painful, costly mistakes along the way that with just a little bit of support, encouragement and good information could have been avoided.

I saw a void I could fill, and that void became an idea I couldn't shake off. Trust me, I tried to avoid it, because who in their right mind starts a business with three children aged five and under? Well, a passionate entrepreneurial type of course. A calculated risk-taker. Me. When my third baby turned one, I decided to create my own business teaching marketing to women entrepreneurs.

In spite of (or perhaps because of) being fully aware of how challenged I was already to manage home clutter, tackle dust bunnies, diminish mountains of laundry and create healthy meals, I took a passionate leap forward into my new venture carefully crafted around the family calendar. With a chicken scratched marketing map, a bit of research, and impeccable instincts (if I do say so myself), I began creating and delivering weekly women's only marketing classes.

I long ago ditched the notion of a 'balanced' life in favour of ways to juggle my way to success - because balance is impossible, life interrupts, dust bunnies last forever, and passion to share my strengths (at home and in the world) is what matters most. This is the story of how I (mostly – other than the mountains of laundry and dust bunnies) succeed as a motivated part-time entrepreneur (even when life kind of sucks - and especially when it doesn't).

Success Ritual 1: Start As You Mean to Carry On – With Passion and Conviction

I said I took a passionate leap forward. And passionate leaps are well, not always practical. On many days, like when the little princesses get sick or the killer dust bunnies finally must be thwarted, when life is more challenging than expected, when business doesn't go quite as planned... it would be easy to quit.

Acknowledging that you started your business with a seed of passion, and always connecting back to that insightful reason, is what carries you through the rollercoaster. Quitting only serves to cause further disappointment. When I lose connection with my passion for my business, usually on day 2 of a migraine or when the hormonal rollercoaster kicks in, I take a peak at the testimonials and comments scattered throughout my website, blog and Facebook page as a reminder why I started in the first place.

The giving of information and inspiration is always returned exponentially. Taking a moment to remember the difference I have made is instant grounding and reconnects me so I can carry one the way I began – with passion and conviction.

Success Ritual 2: Claim What Success Looks Like For You

Life can really throw you lemons... baskets of really sour lemons. I know that to keep my business momentum going, I MUST have parts of my business sustain themselves, because the unexpected eventually happens (guaranteed). And if I'm not careful, my expectations will constantly exceed my abilities. This is a mindset game created in years of corporate life where I had sick days, holidays and no kids and where I had ample time to create success for others. This is NOT my reality any longer, so my definitions of success have slowly adjusted to match my real life which is mostly great (but occasionally sucks!).

Expect the Unexpected

Illness and injuries are the greatest enemies of part-time entrepreneurs. These culprits steal the little bits of time you have set aside for your business. Time you likely can't make up anywhere except in the twilight hours or early mornings. If you've ever had a child, yourself, aging parents or grandparents, or your spouse get moderately or seriously injured or sick, you know what I mean. It can take your business off the rails for weeks and months at a time.

The other unexpected impact on your business is when a work project you've poured your heart into doesn't work out. This can rip focus from your business and make it incredibly difficult to get back on track. I know this happens to everyone. So just know you aren't alone.

Getting in the habit of expecting (and planning for) the unexpected should evolve into your business model. If you can create parts of your business that can stand alone, with help of others, or with minimal use of your time, then you can continue to be in business, even when life tells you otherwise (I use points 6 and 7 below to help me).

Set Mini-Goals as Measures of Success. Here are mine:

1. Create a plan that permits me to have slow and steady growth over a 3-5 period timeline (for me this takes me to the year

my youngest child is in full time school – this is NOT a co-incidence, it's a plan)

2. Use a marketing map – a visual tool that keeps me focused on my goals and how I'll get there (this is a class I offer)

3,. Write down how much time and money I have to invest in my business before I commit to a campaign;

4. Never spend more money than I have, or what I KNOW I will earn within the next 6 weeks, on a campaign – I call this cost-recovery marketing;

5. Realistically assess my 5 other resources – knowledge, network, technology, resources, passion (I also have a class about 7 Essential Resources to being a Part-Time Entrepreneur);

6. Define a realistic monthly revenue target that fits with whatever campaign I am running at the time;

7. Use social media to stay connected (especially when I DON'T have a program running or my business in full swing)

8. Blog meaningful content, regularly to maintain my brand as a 'sharing and caring' marketer;

9. Ensure my children have healthy meals, clean clothes and arrive where they need to be on time;

10 .Get enough sleep (I still don't manage this one often enough);

11. Have at least one date night with my husband a month;

12. Do something fun with my family every week;

13. Do as much as I can with the least amount of childcare possible (this is my personal preference – those who have caregivers helping with kids just get more time and I respect that!)

14. Reward myself often - most of the revenue I make goes back into my business or into my family, however, I ALWAYS reward myself too. Often it's just in the form of a $5 mug of

deliciousness at my favourite coffee stop. And that's enough to remind myself I work hard and deserve rewards for it! And once a year I try to make a weekend away, on a seat sale if need be. In fact, this chapter is being written from the west coast (not my home). I earned this restful reward and am enjoying it.

Being Real About Success

For me, success is really about two things. And I'm certainly not saying I achieve all my success measures, all the time… but knowing what success looks like for me make it much easier to reach it more often!

Here are the two success measures that matter the most:

1. being happy (no matter what lemons life hands me)
2. being the same me in life and in business… no matter what

Success Ritual 3: Acknowledge and Act Like a Part-Time Entrepreneur

If you are a part-time entrepreneur, it is by CHOICE, right? Likely you are busy being a mom, or a caregiver to a family member, or have another job, or volunteer commitments. Eventually you may have the choice because you are making enough money to work part-time as a luxury!

Do yourself a favour. Be honest with others and yourself. You are PART-time. You do not have the ability to say yes to opportunities that a full-time entrepreneur might. Knowing your limitations will benefit your self-care, your other responsibilities, and the quality of your brand. You have made a choice. And choice is a powerful thing. It empowers you to use the time you have wisely.

Claim The Calendar – You Get "Office Hours"

I made the choice to be a part-time entrepreneur, continue to be full-time mom and work my business around the family calendar. Frankly, in my best weeks, I can only claim 5-10 daylight hours of my week for my business around that epic family calendar. This never feels like enough, but it does keep me grounded to my family values. It also ensures everyone knows my commitment to my business is tangible and real. It IS in the calendar after all!

How much time do you really have?

A part-time entrepreneur may actually work full-time hours. I know I do… in the wee hours of the night after everyone is finally asleep and I find some solitude. But those wee hours don't count. That is not a sustainable business model. (Trust me, I know this.) So how much time do you REALLY have in daylight hours to work semi-uninterrupted (yes, letting the kids watch a movie while you work can be "real office hours")? If it's less than 30, you are a part-time entrepreneur.

For self-preservation and business success, you have to follow different rules to success than your full-time entrepreneurial friends. Consider these

5 realities that suck about entrepreneurial life:

1. Never enough time to create and act on all your ideas

2. Never enough money to get the ball rolling as fast as you'd like

3. The rest of your life (the part that stops you from being a full time entrepreneur) always takes priority and can interrupt your business life

4. You are a step away from being a non-entrepreneur often (being that making money and not is the difference)

5. Life can you hand you lemons, and if they are big ones, they can really impact your business momentum

5 rewards of part-time entrepreneurial life:

1. Choice to take care of your other responsibilities as much as required

2. Freedom from your other responsibilities for a little while

3. Unlimited opportunity to succeed over time

4. Slow and steady growth benefit to your long-term business

5. You get to be a role model and make a difference in big ways on limited resources

Success Ritual 4: Develop and Maintain a Brand Personality That Fits Like a Glove

About 8 months after launching my marketing classes at local community halls, I realized I was reaching enough success, at a rapid enough rate, that I was already able to expand. Since I couldn't clone myself, I had to find a new way to reach more people.

One attempt was to align with like-minded business professionals. I had one major success in forming an alliance with a colleague who is part of my constant support system. Another attempt at collaboration was a brutal failure. It was the one time when I didn't listen to my instincts, and it took me quickly down a rabbit hole that without quick action would have damaged my brand. Fortunately, I had built a loyal and understanding following, having been a visible, consistent role model from the beginning. So to save my brand, I had to talk about my failure as a learning opportunity.

What followed was, and continues to be, amazing. My credibility as a truth-telling marketer has defined my brand. And from that experience I've evolved directly into online marketing to grow my business in a more sustainable way.

The First $2500 I Spent Mattered the Most

A brand is core to success, no matter how you define success. And brand, for a part-time entrepreneur, is typically built on infusing your business with your personality in a consistent way. In my case, since I've taken on sharing marketing solutions for women similar to me, sharing my personal stories mattered very much.

After my collaboration failure, I gave a hard-look at my strengths and capabilities and shifted my mind fully into the possibilities of integrating traditional and online marketing for my business, and for my clients. I invested my first $2500 I earned into creating a professional logo, visual identity and WordPress site I could manage myself. Other than some supporting online coaching classes *(from Gina Bell, author of this book)* and the purchase of some technology tools, $2500 is all I've spent on my business and it's all I've needed to create the visibility and credibility I enjoy today (that is growing exponentially).

Finding My Voice and Sharing The Real Me Online

I evolved my brand voice from face-to-face live classes to include the written word and international online relationships through tweets, Facebook sharing, webinars and blogging.

I have built a brand on being real, sharing loads of extremely useful free content, and acting like a normal imperfect human being who happens to have some great marketing common sense and credentials.

Success Ritual 5: Use Every Experience as Market Research & Growth Opportunity

When I did an inventory of my early phase of business, I realized that marketing instincts, as much as marketing knowledge, had been guiding me. I considered the live classes in local community halls as incubators of insight into the lives of other women part-time entrepreneurs.

Learn What You Can and Then Move On

My weekly marketing class model was incredibly popular. It was immensely rewarding, and I consider the two years of those programs to be significant in building my visibility and credibility. However, as the classes grew in popularity and as much as I valued the richness of face-to-face classes, I had to admit they weren't fully successful by my definitions of success – they were impacting my family life more than I wanted. Without cloning myself (why haven't we discovered how to do that yet?), it became an unsustainable business model.

So, I used the rich insight and experience of having been face to face with these women entrepreneurs as key market research to investigate new ideas and ways to share my knowledge and my passion, while maintaining success on my terms.

Growth Is Painful, But Rewarding

Redefining 'how to grow' was a very bumpy road filled with significant disappointment. I had thought if I can't clone myself, then maybe I could collaborate and spread my advocacy and teaching of women entrepreneurs in partnership with others. In theory, it is still the most exceptional way to grow and succeed and share common philosophies. But it doesn't always work, as I already pointed out.

Eventually I accepted my first FAIL in business collaboration was not the failure of my business in general but rather was a first step in discovering other growth ideas. (And this is when I had the light bulb that slow and steady growth was often better after all). After choosing not to quit altogether, I dug a bit deeper and did create a more sustainable (sometimes) business model blending online and face-to-face programs that fit with my real life.

Success Ritual 6: Cultivate and Cull Relationships

I could call this section "Everything I Know About Business Relationships I Learned in High School". Do you remember aspiring to be in the 'cool kid group' at school but not knowing why? Or wanting to be friends with someone because they had a certain quality you knew you'd never have, even though on some level you knew doing so would be a really bad idea? Business is like that too! In this era of pervasive 'relationship building' it is easy to feel attracted to the most popular networking groups and most dynamic leaders. It is normal to feel a sense of awe and fear of your competition. And it is easy to begin building enthusiastic relationships, sharing ideas and starting plans with another when caught up in the momentum of popularity and initial attraction. But wait… this isn't high school and guess what… seeking popularity over real relationships didn't work then either.

"Get Thousands of Followers A Day" Simply Gets My Goat

My experience from high school to now, except for a few missteps, has been pretty much built on authentic relationship building. Not the buzzword variety of "authentic". I mean, I am blessed to have very close friends, most entrepreneurial, who have known me since I was 13! And other close business relationships have been built on having a true sense of who really fits with me.

Building business is NOT a popularity contest. And experts who claim they can "get you thousands of new [Facebook or Twitter or email] followers a day" (for a fee, fyi), really get my goat. Can you imagine building thousands of new MEANINGFUL relationships a day? Do you think you can discover who is a meaningful potential customer or collaborator if you had a thousand new people to build friendships with each day?

I didn't think so. Seeking fewer relationships of higher quality in all areas of business and life (online and in real life) is far more manageable, satisfying and eventually financially rewarding in nearly every instance. The only time having thousands of new followers a day makes sense is if you have a product or service that is so universally appealing, in limited supply and high demand, that relationships don't matter. But a business model where relationships don't matter isn't a good model is it?

You Only Have Time to Build Meaningful Relationships

Cultivating the right relationships and culling the wrong ones is the difference between building a band of brand champions who can propel you forward or staying stagnant in a sea of uninterested or competitive colleagues. Imagine ditching your comfortable high school best friend, who has your back no matter what, to go to a party with a bunch of high school colleagues who don't give a rats patooty about you (or you about them) because that's where the "cool kids" are. You wouldn't, right? That's stuff for John Hughes movies, not for real life or real business. (For the record, I never ditched a friend to go to a party... this is a lesson I didn't have to learn the hard way).

Set goals to reach 1000 meaningful new relationships every six months and you will be on your way to part-time entrepreneurial success.

Success Ritual 7: Celebrate Success and Practice Patience

Being a part-time entrepreneur is not going to work for someone deeply affected by rejection, by being on the sidelines more than the limelight, or someone needing to make big money fast.

I have been blessed to have had my photo and story in the Globe & Mail, I've been promoted on Twitter by Canadian business celebrities. I rank strongly on social media as an advocate, supporter and connector. I make money. My Credibility, Visibility, Sellability© grow exponentially each year. My star is still on the rise. Weekly I must celebrate the small indicators that I'm making a mark with the little bit of time each week I have.

Every small success spurs me on to imagine bigger and better ways to grow my business. But I simply can't. My success measure is being happy and being me – and that stems from staying mom to my kids more than devotee to my own business. So I have to practice patience in my rate of growth. Tough, but it keeps all my values in check.

Success Ritual 8: Change Scenery, Change Perspective

The hardest thing about being a multi-tasking, motivated, Type A part-time entrepreneur is getting focused fast. Being able to shift gears from mom-taxi driver to cook to housekeeper to entrepreneur on a dime is critical. Taking a break from my home office or finding a new view causes an enlightened change of perspective that inspires me fastest into action.

I've been known to reference "my Starbucks office" where I literally leave home to go work for a few hours each week. At times I actually remove myself from my home office and home life for a longer period of time, like a weekend. I try to make an annual weekend trip away by myself to catch up on sleep, ideas and gain some solitude. This weekend resets my motivation. Not to mention lets me sleep in!

Finding daily, weekly, monthly and annual ways to reconnect with the passionate drive behind business is the number one success ritual for part-time entrepreneurs. Without it, your business may not last.

Where it often takes a full time entrepreneur 2-3 years to realize the full success they are seeking, a part-time entrepreneur may take 3-5 (or more). And this is okay. This is your choice. Own it. Take care of yourself. Be smart with your time and money. Don't make excuses, make success rituals, and you can make your business success happen!

About the Author: Affordable. Useful. Fun. Easy. Effective. Trusted. This is how Kim's approach and advice is described by her fans as she mentors, motivates and educates about small business marketing. Through her company MPowered Marketing, and as Founder of International Alliance of Motivated Part-Time Entrepreneurs, Kim is on a mission. With workshops, coaching and connecting people to the right information or other experts, she is committed to helping small business owners make exceptional marketing choices no matter how limited their resources. Join Kim's mission at www.mpoweredmarketing.com or at www.iampte.com, the world's only community dedicated to supporting success of part-time business owners.

Dump the Junk that's Holding You Back and Make Room for Success

KIMBERLY ENGLOT

"Success isn't a result of spontaneous combustion. You must set yourself on fire."

– Arnold H. Glasow

I used to have a lot of junk. Junk in my home, Junk in my body and Junk in my mind. The Junk took many forms: not taking care of myself, people-pleasing, tolerating abusive employers, and panic disorder. I gained 30 pounds over six months and anger was taking over my relationships.

I complained to anyone who would listen about my under-employment, lack of money and lack of connections or opportunity. I was a mess and as you can imagine very pleasant to be around (note my sarcasm).

In late 2007, I had a light-bulb moment that made me turn my life around. I had a mirror experience where I saw myself the way my husband saw me (as a hate-filled, angry woman) and I didn't like it. That was enough to get me to take a good hard look at who I had become and who I actually wanted to be.

I didn't know my authentic self. I couldn't feel anything but pain. I needed a major spirit overhaul, to get down to the core of what I wanted. I need to discover my authentic self.

It happened slowly. About six months after my light-bulb moment I jumped on "The Secret" bandwagon (two years late, but better late than never) and life started to get really good after that. This point, in early 2008 is where I started to actually "get it" and my success ritual was born.

Identifying the Junk

The Secret opened my eyes to a whole new world. Up until then, I had been very analytic and science-based. (I still am, but I'm way more open minded and tolerant now, not to mention happier!)

I looked at my life and I didn't like what I saw. It was full of people who used me, abused me and stole my dreams. They had to go.

I wasn't taking good care of myself, and my Doctor was concerned about my weight gain. The lack of self-care had to go.

I wasn't nourishing my passion and my love of psychology and people was dying…the depression that followed had to go.

I was holding onto old clothes, old books, old memories and they all had to go!

I was full of mindset Junk; excuses, victim story, fear, anger, guilt, perfection…that all had to go.

And I had to forgive and release some pain from my past.

Releasing the Junk

Over the next year I dumped a lot of junk. And I turned my life completely around almost a year to the day of my initial light-bulb moment. I flexed my bounce-back muscles, exercised my happiness muscles and my life that had atrophied from the anger started to bloom. The first person to notice was my husband. My close friends and family noticed next and my world has expanded to be filled with joy, peace and trust in a way that I never thought was possible, only a few years ago.

The process that I went through became the curriculum for my signature program, The Master Life Cleanse and now I see that that all of the Junk that had accumulated was a gift in disguise because it helped me grow and help others.

What is the Junk?

One thing I learned is that Junk sneaks up when you're not looking. If you don't continually take out the garbage, it will overflow, then pile up and then take over! It's the same with life and you have to continually be aware of what you let in (and let stay) or the Junk will take over.

Whenever I notice that something doesn't feel right in my business, Junk, is to blame. There might be a toxic person, holding me back. There might be some Automatic Negative Thoughts, or limiting beliefs holding me hostage. There might be lack of clarity, focus or priorities keeping me stuck.

Whatever it is, it's Junk, and so it must go.

Wiping Away the Top Layer

One of my favourite metaphors is something I first learned from Success Coach, Michael Neill. In his book, *Supercoach*:

"A friend of mine once put it, we're like diamonds who have spent so much time applying layer upon layer of nail polish to appear beautiful to the world that we begin to believe we must be covered in horse crap."

You are a diamond, and you have spent so much time trying to be perfect for others, that you forgot you were a diamond. When you didn't live up to their expectations, or when their obligations weighed heavy on your spirit, you thought it was your fault. You thought you were a failure and you thought that you were horse crap.

You are not horse crap. You are perfect. Success and happiness are yours for the taking when you realize that and dump the Junk that it telling you otherwise.

It's time to strengthen your awareness (aka: the ability to know where the answers are coming from; the Ego or the Authentic Self) and your ability to see yourself as successful.

To begin the Junk dumping process, wipe away the first layer with the following exercise.

Ask yourself a few questions:

- What do I want in life?

- What is my passion?

- What am I willing to do to get what I want?

- What am I NOT willing to do to get what I want?

- What has been holding me back?

- What do I view as my purpose in life?

The more of these kinds of questions you ask, the closer you get to your authentic self, the more Junk you dump . Good questions will give you the clarity that is necessary for you to determine whether your resistance to change/opportunity is coming from irrational fear (fake fear or the ego saying, "I'm uncomfortable") or rational fear (danger awareness which is your intuition saying, "This is a BAD idea and you are in physical danger").

Get over the fake fear, achieve the clarity and gain the power that you need to succeed in your business (and life).

To go a step further and dump the Junk, take cues from your body. As you are answering the questions from the exercise above be aware of the following:

Be aware of your emotions. Did you all-of-a-sudden feel a surge of anger? Where did that come from? Is there something making you stressed or on edge? What?

Don't spend days dwelling on any uncomfortable feelings, but if necessary journal for 10 minutes on any strong emotions that come up.

Be aware of your body. Did you go from feeling good, to wanting to cry? Were you relaxed a few moments ago and now you're tense and gritting your teeth?

Your physical reactions will always guide you to what is really going on, assuming you stop to notice. Often people don't realize they have stopped breathing or have tensed up until they gasp for air or get a headache.

Be aware of your instincts. The stomach is the center of everything; many people can literally feel in their gut that something isn't right. Listen to that feeling because your intuition picks up these shifty vibes. Your solar plexus chakra is in your gut and it picks up this energy.

If there are times when you walk into a room and can't wait to leave (for no rational reason) or when you meet someone who you automatically don't trust, it's your instincts making themselves known. It's too bad that often instead of listening to these intuitive nudges, we discount them as being prejudiced or mean. I know that I have been burned many times in the past, getting a strong urgency to distance myself from someone and not listening only to find out the hard way later on. Let's just say I have learned my lesson and I listen to my instincts without worrying about hurting a stranger's feelings.

This is the beginning in a long line of ways that I dump my Junk, but it is the start that I need to keep me grounded, happy and healthy. I am aligned with my authentic self now, happier than I've ever been, and more successful, prosperous and abundant than I ever thought possible.

Life is good!

About the Author: Kimberly Englot is the founder of The Center for Authentic Self Development. She teaches women how to go from Desperate Housewives to Deliberately Happy, without feeling guilty or selfish. Creator of the Master Life Cleanse system, and author of The Now of Happiness: Your Official Happiness Formula, she knows her happiness formula, has loads of energy and a zest for life.

She currently lives in Canada with her husband, Chris, and fur babies: Nixie and Maxx. You are most likely to find her snuggled up reading a book or writing!

Learn more at http://KimberlyEnglot.com

What's the Point If You Can't Dance?

KIVA LEATHERMAN

My ritual for success? Integrating everything, and I mean everything, into my work, and **making sure that I've created a business that allows me to be me:** a little hyper, a little crazy, fun and fiercely positive. That's not to say there aren't aspects of my work that I have to fight with myself tooth and nail on, like QuickBooks! I can be a procrastination queen. But because I've built a business I love, I have plenty of fuel to burn through the drudge work. And what I love to do, more than anything in the world, is to teach women to dance. It just took me a while to figure out that was what my business was actually about.

Have you ever just decided to give up on being great? I did – quite purposefully. I was 16 years old and I'd been dancing since – well, forever. My mom came to find her passion for dance later in life and she was going to make sure I didn't have to wait quite so long. I grew up in New York, and so had access to some pretty incredible teachers and schools. And by the time I was 16… I was great.

But that felt like a lot of pressure. And expectation. And auditions! I hated auditions – because I wasn't always the great-est. And so I quit, In my mind at least. I danced for a few more years into college, and then, I quit letting my body dance.

I decided that it would be much more fun to be ordinary – as ordinary as I could make myself, anyway, having been reminded by my Mom constantly, that I was actually extraordinary. Not just because I danced, but because I was smart, and independent and I could take care of myself. She taught me so well, but I decided in my infinite wisdom that she was wrong. I decided that the real key to happiness was to act just like everyone else.

So I worked at being ordinary for a very long time. I did not excel in college. Despite my best efforts at ordinary, I did reasonably well in my career in the mutual fund industry, advancing quickly. Since it was the end of the greatest bull market in history, I did very well financially, too. I was very good at it – I loved the speed of it, and giving presentations. I enjoyed the beginning especially, in that steep curve of learning a whole new language and a whole new world. I enjoyed the journey to becoming an expert.

But after 10 years or so I was bored. I still did well. But to be honest, I could have done so much more. Always squeaking by and always doing the least amount of work possible, I held on. And I made it look like I was enjoying myself.

The bitter truth is that I was so sad during that time. On the outside, and I'm sure to all of my friends and family looking in it looked like I'd lived up to my potential, and that I'd fulfilled my Mom's promise that I was extraordinary.

But to me, it all felt like a big, fat lie. I guess it was. And eventually that lie caught up to me. Hating your job does not inspire your best work (as I'm sure many of you can relate) and I got fired.

So I faked being happy that I got fired. I told myself and everyone else that it was ideal, that all I wanted was to be a mommy. I actually had two young children at the time – and I was genuinely grateful to have the opportunity to spend time with them. But I was not fulfilled. They are wonderful - and a huge part of my purpose, but they are just a piece of my puzzle.

I spent a lot of time watching television in those years. I taught myself to crochet. And I got certified to become an aerobics instructor. I started teaching a dance class at my local gym, teaching women simple choreography to amazing music. In that gym, with those women, my heart soared. I mean, I felt elation like I've never felt before in my life… as an aerobics instructor. Wait… I'm supposed to be extraordinary.

"Well, this can't be it," I thought, "I can't have been put on this earth to be an aerobics instructor!"

So I thought some more and contemplated my future. I seriously had no idea who I was, or what I was "supposed" to do. I just knew I had to figure it out, because sitting home and watching my children grow up, waiting for the bus to come home and chauffeuring them to soccer and ballet wasn't going to do it for me. I crocheted, and thought some more and watched a ridiculous amount of T.V. One day, while doing all of the above, it came to me. Like a bolt of energy that shot down through my brain and into my body, I knew what I had to do. I figured if I could take what I loved about teaching women to dance, and combine it with what I knew about investing and business, that I would be able to have an incredible business teaching women about their money and about living up to their worth.

Another success ritual? **Act with speed.** I'd been thinking about how to spend my time when my children were off to school, which was a couple of years away at that point, but I was so excited by my idea that I started right away. I called an old co-worker, my partner Julie, who is an amazing trainer and coach. I knew I lacked expertise in that area (success ritual number three: know your strengths and seek help on everything else). A few weeks later we signed the incorporation paperwork at a local playground, while our children enjoyed a play date. Wise Workshops was born.

We started offering local workshops to teach women to succeed with their money, their health and their time. And it went o.k., but I realized that I had a lot to learn. I realized that there were no short cuts to be taken in building a business. And I realized that there was no faking it, no squeaking by, and that hanging up fliers around coffee shops in my community was probably not the most effective marketing plan. I realized with astounding clarity that in order to teach women to live up to their worth and reach their potential that I better start living up to mine.

I dug in, and sought to immerse myself in learning about online marketing, and operations, and information publishing and technology. I read everything I could get my hands on about teaching women, and learning about the challenges that women face in their careers, families and with the competing requirements on their time. I became passionate about empowering women in third world countries to learn about entrepreneurship and attended conferences with incredibly amazing women doing incredibly amazing work in the world.

For the first time in my life, I was demanding excellence of myself. I was really busy. And I was spending a lot of money and not making any. Well, except for the $15/hour that I made teaching my aerobics class.

I started to have a conversation with myself that went something like this:

"Wow, Kiva, you are really busy and you are not making any money."

"Something is not working."

"Maybe it's because all of your creative juices are being used up for your dance class and not for your business."

"Maybe you should quit teaching your dance class."

The next week, in front of 40 women – I blew out my ACL, in a spectacular crash landing out of this spinning jumping thing that I was trying to show-off… which if you know anything about knees, means I was done – dancing – and maybe for good. Ouch.

I knew right away I'd have my knee fixed and go through the rehab, and that I would be back teaching as soon as they let me. I needed to have my passion taken away to learn deep in my heart that I couldn't give it up. For me, I soar when I dance and when I see the women in my class moving and shaking and laughing and sweating and being amazing.

In the time that I had during my recuperation I did a lot of writing and a lot of working on the marketing and messaging of what I wanted Wise Workshops to be. I knew that I wanted to teach women to be successful with their money, their health and their time. I knew I wanted women to believe that they can be whatever and have whatever they want. I knew that it was vital that women have the education, means and resources to be self-reliant, not to depend on anyone else for their financial, emotional and physical well being. I knew that I wanted women to know that through engagement and action they can have an immediate impact on issues in our world. I knew that I wanted women to thrive. And suddenly, it came to me. Wise teaches women to DANCE.

Our process became the acronym D.A.N.C.E . – Decide – Accept – kNow – Commit – Expand, to teach women to achieve their goals – regardless of whether they are financial, emotional, physical or career goals, these are the steps that we teach for success. But the coolest part is that when I'm giving a talk or teaching a workshop, I literally teach the attendees to dance! I've had lunch seminars up and boogie-ing around the table and college women coming together to learn choreography – moving and shaking and laughing and sweating and being amazing and LEARNING.

The crazy thing is – once DANCE became a part of our lexicon and what we do at Wise – everything began to come together in crazy cool ways. Speaking opportunities materialized, partnerships became easy. Even time management came easier, since I know that I am on the right path, I am more present for my family, making sure to have time just for them, no cell phone allowed!

If you can figure out how to design your work so that it is so incredibly rewarding and connected to who you are, and allows you to do things that make your heart soar – suddenly work doesn't feel the same. Things that used to feel tedious have purpose. I like to say that you know that you're on the right path when you do what is necessary, even if it's really, really hard.

I think the key is to stop thinking about the aspects of your life as separate and conflicting demands on your resources and to begin to consider, ritualistically, how you can integrate those pieces into your very own beautiful puzzle. As an entrepreneur, you have an incredible opportunity to create whatever you want. There are no rules. There are no limitations. You can become one of the privileged few that get to do exactly what you were made to do. You get to design your life.

So that you can soar, and you can be wise and you can dance.

About the Author: Kiva Leatherman is the Founder and President of Wise Workshops, which develops curriculum for women to learn about their health, wealth and time. As a speaker, she encourages women to know themselves, to know about their money and to stop living vicariously through others – to achieve success and happiness on their terms.

Her personal mission is to ensure that women are in charge of their own money, their own time and the decisions that they make regarding their nutrition and health. She teaches women to create a framework for success which gives them the power and freedom to live well.

Learn more about Kiva and her work at www.WiseWorkshops.com

Taming the Chaos of
Information Overload

Laura Lee Sparks

We all have the same 24 hours in a day, 7 days in a week, 24 hours in a day, 60 minutes in an hour yet we are all different in how we spend it. Note the word "spend". We spend time, just as we spend money. But most us never think of time as we do money.

As women entrepreneurs, we juggle so many things both professionally and personally and due to technology it never feels like we can escape information overload. A key success ritual is learning how to tame the chaos of information both in our business and in our personal lives because for most us, one leads into the other, and we don't traditionally clock in out of either work or home life.

We live in a world where we are constantly bombarded with information: emails, social media, instant messages, cell phones, office phones, home phones, text messages, snail mail, and the list goes on. Most of us try to keep up with all of this as it comes in, talking on the phone while reading email, reading email while talking to a staff member, checking out social media sites during meetings, and the list goes on….stop.this.now.

When you are trying to do more than one thing at a time you are going to make more mistakes, you are going to spend more time, and you are going drive yourself crazy.

You are one person, and you only have 24 hours in a day. You can only do one thing at a time and do it well. And when you try to do more you are short changing yourself, your business, your staff, your family or whomever else is directly or indirectly affected by your multitasking.

You can not give **quality** attention to more than one thing at one time, and anything that deserves your attention deserves your quality attention (if it doesn't why are you giving it any of your attention? Remember time is spent and you can't get it back so let's be mindful of what we give our time to).

Just like we borrow money, many of us try to borrow time. When you borrow time, you pay interest at a much higher level than you do when you borrow money. For instance, statistics say when you borrow an hour of sleep you must get two hours of sleep to make up for it that is 100% interest!

When you borrow time from your family, the interest you pay is much higher especially depending on who or what you are borrowing from.

The techniques that I'm going to discuss need to become part of your life, both personally and professionally and when you implement them you will begin to see a shift: both in more time available, more productivity and most importantly better relationships with your staff and your family.

We talked above about all the "stuff" that is coming at us all day long. Now let's talk about what to do with all of it.

What I have found in my own life and working with clients is that we all have lots of gathering places. When we talk about gathering places we are talking about all those places that we put things:

multiple email boxes, piles in the office, piles in the car, our purse or briefcase, piles in the house, next to the bed, desk drawers, cork boards, physical inboxes, calendars, notepads, text messages, to do lists, post it notes, journals, computer desktop screen, the list goes on and you get my drift it is a lot of places.

Then there is your MIND. It can become the biggest cluster of all when you try to depend on it to "remember" things, especially when you have a multitude of other gathering places that it can't help but go to even when you do not want it to. It's just the nature of how the mind works. It knows that there are piles, and that there may be time bombs sitting in there, so it is going to go to those places and you are going to be spending or borrowing time that doesn't need to spent if those places were narrowed down.

Think about your surroundings both at the office and at home and think about how many gathering places you have. Now, let's narrow that down. This is going to give you back more time than you will ever imagine and you will thank me – if you implement it.

The magic number is 6. Six approved gather places where EVERYTHING will go until it is processed, we'll talk about processing and what that means in a little while.

Gathering Places:

Approved gathering place #1 is **AN** email in box. Not five email inboxes - just one. You can have multiple email accounts but they should all come into one inbox and if you check mail from more than one device all devices must be synced.

The second approved gathering place is going to be a physical inbox. This is papers, mail, memos, notes, books, magazines; anything that you get that must be dealt with during the course of a week. It should be large enough to handle short term storage for the things that you typically need your attention – depending on your business this could vary but for most of my clients and most service professionals one of those legal size wire baskets seem to do the trick.

The third approved gathering place is a portable inbox, this is going to be something you can carry with you just about anywhere you go, it's important because we collect "stuff" when we are out and about and if we don't gather it and get it to a place to process it, it will accumulate not just in an unapproved gathering place but also in our mind because it has not been dealt with. Examples of a portable inbox are planners with a zipped pouch, a file folder, one pocket of a briefcase, it should be something that you can easy "dump" into your physical inbox as soon as you get to the office or workspace. Keep in mind the types of things you usually gather, and make the size work for you. I suggest having it be at least letter size so that you do not need to fold papers. Always empty your portable inbox into your physical inbox daily.

The fourth gathering place is voice mail. We all have voice mail, and usually several home, office, cell what you want to do is consolidate as much as possible. There are services that will forward your voice mail to email some that even transcribe them for you. That is my preference but use what works for you trying to get it to where there is only one if possible.

Fifth gathering place is going to be a notepad that you can carry with you. When you have ideas, or some one gives you information, or anything else you need to know and keep track of you are going to write it in your notebook. Here's a few tips, get a notebook that is a comfortable size for you to carry around with you and that has pages you an easily rip out. Write one idea or note per page. When you are at your physical inbox you are going to rip all page of your notebook and deposit into your physical inbox.

Six gathering place is a wildcard. Everyone has their own systems in their business and most of what I am going share in this book is not technology specific. I want you to work with what you are already using in your business and what is already working for you. I want the process of getting more streamlined and productive to be easy not halted by a learning curve. With that said, you probably use some sort of task list, to do list, list on your phone, project management tool on your computer, an iPhone gadget or iPad gadget, whatever it may be that you add information to that you need to come back to later to look at or do something with. You pick what it is for you.

Once in while I'll work with a client who has to have seven gathering places and that is ok too. The idea is to keep it limited to 6-8 and here is the most important part. You are going to process each gathering place to ZERO at least once per week.

Processing – the W-W-W

Now that you have approved gathering places what do you do with the "stuff" that gathers in them? We are going to process it, at **scheduled times**.

Scheduled time means that it is on your calendar not in your head. For most of us, I recommend 2 times (short periods) for processing each day, maybe three for email depending on how much email you receive and whether or not you have an assistant that helps manage that. I recommend one longer period once per week for making sure that every gathering place is all the way to empty (yes that means ZERO).

Yes, I said three times for email, if you want to get productive you must not live out of your inbox, or stay connected to it via your cell phone. I know so many business owners who are just trapped in the pit of thinking that they have to jump every time an email arrives. Most of us are not in businesses where there are life and death situations, emergencies account for probably 1% of your email in a given year. Let your clients and staff know your policies for checking email and come up with a solution for the 1% of time that it truly is something that needs to be handled immediately.

Rules for Processing

Obviously you are not going to be able complete every project and idea that lands in a gathering point every week. Remember you are only one person. The point of processing is to get it out of a gathering point and get it on the schedule.

We'll use the **W-W- W formula** to sort through everything in a gathering place.

- **W**hat is the next step
- **W**hen will it be done
- **W**here does the item live

What is the next step?

Everything has a next step, an email may need a response, a business card may need to be added to a contact list, a contract may need to be reviewed, an article may need to be written. Using the rules above determine if you will do this now, add it to a task list or schedule it on a calendar.

Notice I'm not saying what task list, or calendar. I want you to use what you are comfortable with, what you are used to working with or what your team is used to working it. It's not about the technology its about the system and the creating the **habit of following the system.**

When is it going to be done?

The standard to follow for this is not when the entire project will be done, but when the next step will happen, (the what) here are some other handy rules for processing the when:

- If it will take less than 2 minutes do it now right while you are processing
- If it will take 15 minutes or less and is NOT time sensitive add it to task list
- If it will take more than 15 minutes or IS time sensitive calendar it

All things that are on task lists and of course on the calendar should have a date associated with them. Tasks will not have a time but should have a date. Calendared items have both. When scheduling on the calendar I suggest not scheduling things back to back, give yourself leeway for a call that may run over, a task that may take a little longer, and of course travel time if there is travel involved. Remember there are only 24 hours in your day so plan your schedule so that you do not have to borrow time.

The last thing to determine as you are processing is Where.

Where does this object "live", where is it's home until you do your next step?

None of your gathering places is ever a home. Once something is processed it can not go back into your inbox.

Some examples of where you could place physical things are stacking trays on your desk, you may have a tray for calendared items to do, and waiting for additional information, files in the drawer of your desk could serve this purpose as well.

Your where's need to be labeled and accessible based upon how often you will use them. If it is something you will need to access daily it should be at or very close to your desk, if it is weekly, monthly or longer it can be placed further away.

Creating a system of limiting the number of gathering places, processing them daily and getting them to zero at least once a week will free you like nothing else on this planet. You will no longer be wondering "what has fallen off my radar" or feeling like you are tip-toeing through a mine field.

Remember a good habit takes 21 days to create, the more you do this and stick with it the easier it is going to be and the less time it is going to require of you to do the processing.

Once you begin to successfully filter and process the information that is coming at you both professional and personally you will tame the chaos of information overload and be amazed that the time you have freed up!

About the Author: Laura Lee Sparks is a woman on a mission to share the simple solution of productivity, management, marketing and systems to professional services providers allowing them to discover how grow their businesses, make more money, and have plenty of personal time to enjoy their life.

As a reformed paralegal and office manager for a multi lawyer law firm, she has built two successful six figure online businesses of her own, and served as EVP for a company that went from launch to over a million dollars in revenue in 18 months.

She, along with her rock star team at The Simple Solution are bringing her savvy, sassy, down-to-earth secrets for creating "Success and a Life"™ to burned-out professional service entrepreneurs nationwide through exclusive training programs, products and coaching services.

More about Laura Lee at http://thesimplesolution.com/

The Unintended Ritual
(and a Few I Planned)

KIM DOYAL

In an ideal world, all the rituals we have that get us to where we want to be would be well thought out plans, created with the best of intentions and followed to a "T". But the ideal world doesn't really exist and isn't nearly as rewarding as the real world, even with all the bumps and bruises we gather along the way.

What's most surprising is that the success rituals I've created have evolved somewhat organically. The reason I say "surprising" is because I think the assumption with a ritual is that it is a conscious, well-thought-out, structured task that is implemented with the best of intentions. Sometimes they are and sometimes they aren't. My experience has been that through trial and error I've created rituals that not only drive my business, but keep me grounded (and sane!).

Before getting into the specifics of my own success rituals, I think it's important for any business owner to make the decision from day ONE that you know how you work best (in other words, trust your gut). With the amount of information available it's easy to feel that maybe someone else has a better system, methodology or structure to running a business. I'm not saying you shouldn't try other ways of doing things, getting organized, etc., but if you know you're someone who prefers using a day runner or physical calendar- it doesn't make sense to spend your time setting up an online calendar system. Personally, I tend to mix old school and new school. Some things are digital and some things are paper- it just depends on what I'm doing. Most of the time when I've tried a different way of doing things- I end up feeling like I've created a 'job' for myself or feeling resentful.

Business Rituals

My success rituals definitely fall into both business and personal rituals, with some falling into both categories. I think most business owners will tell you that your rituals will change and evolve as your business does, so keep in mind that what works for you when you're first starting out may not work for you 3 years later. Probably THE most important ritual that has evolved in my business is one that is also very applicable in my personal life, and that would be creating a way in which I am accountable.

Accountability: Initially when I realized that I worked better by setting up some sort of a 'checks and balances' in my business, I felt like it was a weakness. It seemed very counter intuitive that I would be an entrepreneur but needed to be held accountable? This was one of those areas where I needed to step back, get out of my head and simply observe what was working. Once I changed the way I looked at using accountability in my business (as something that I did for myself as a way to get closer to my goals) it became very easy to implement in multiple areas of my business.

The two ways in which I implemented this were through collaboration with other people and by having someone I checked in with on a weekly basis. The first method, through collaboration, was set up with people I was working with on a specific project. We had a business relationship through a different project and I approached them with an idea for something else. While we would be collaborating on the production side of things, getting the project started and making the initial connections were all up to me. And honestly, it was totally frightening! I was stepping out into a new 'arena' and putting myself out there in a really big way. But because I had made a commitment to the people I was collaborating with I knew that when I said I was going to do something I needed to do it. And they followed up with me. Accountability doesn't work if it's just one sided. Once this project was under way and I started getting responses from the people I was reaching out to, I knew there was no turning back.

The other method, my weekly check in, really came from a very personal place. For quite some time when I was working with clients I would end up doing WAY more than the proposal stated or was agreed upon (and this was after tweaking my proposal a zillion times) and would feel very resentful. I had created a problem where I was the source of the issue! The more work I did for other people (that they weren't paying for) the less time I had to work on my OWN projects.

The challenge in this situation is that when you're the person creating the problem, you have a harder time finding the solution. I realized that the best way to address this would be to have an accountability partner who would hold me accountable while being honest and direct with me. This person happened to be someone that had a significant role in my personal life, but wasn't so close to me that they would let me off the hook or were afraid of being honest.

If you think having an accountability partner would help you, I can't stress enough that you need to look for someone who is a step beyond where you are or is someone you KNOW will be direct with you and you don't want to let down. I've tried setting up accountability systems with friends who are on a similar path or are at the same level, and I can tell you in NEVER works. Its way too easy to help each other justify why you didn't complete your previous week's commitments. It only took once for this person to tell me that "while things will come up in your business, for the most part, you're in control of your time" to realize that I was making excuses.

So, here are some suggestions to make accountability work:

- Through collaboration

- Set definitive deadlines for tasks

- Follow up. Ensure you have to answer to your partners

- Set milestones: when developing a project, create milestones that must be completed in order to progress to the next step.

- Find an accountability partner

- Choose someone who is at a level you aspire to or someone who you KNOW you'll follow through with

- Set up a regular time when you will check in with this person

- Be honest! If you're not willing to be honest, you're wasting your time AND theirs!

Keep learning: Being somewhat of an information junkie, this isn't really an area that I have difficulty with, but can easily be put aside because it doesn't 'feel' like work (which, fortunately, most of the time what I do doesn't feel like work).

I tend to be a bit of a multi-tasker (aren't most women?), so am usually reading a few books at a time, as well as going through a course or listening to an audio program. How I implement what I'm learning depends on the subject matter. Some things need to be applied immediately while other things are concepts that need to sink in.

One aspect of my 'learning' ritual is that I subscribe to a few feeds, have them on my iGoogle homepage and start my day by reading the latest post. This ritual is most successful when I engage through blog commenting, re-tweeting or sharing through facebook (hint: make sure when you leave comments on blogs that your brand or title is part of your name. Ex: whenever I leave a comment, my name shows as "Kim Doyal – The WordPress Chick". This one little tip increased traffic through my comments significantly).

One of the biggest benefits of continuing to learn while building your online business isn't necessarily something you can measure. For me, it keeps me excited, motivated and inspired to reach my goals and set the bar higher.

Personal Rituals

Like most entrepreneurs, my business and personal life seem to meld into one most of the time. I wish I could tell you that I've mastered the art of balancing both, but I haven't. Not sure I'm even really close to finding the right balance. But I've finally learned to recognize when I'm out of balance and am getting better at bringing myself back into balance quicker.

Exercise: Yes, kind of obvious I know, but it truly keeps me sane! I have a pretty consistent schedule of exercise and have learned not to schedule appointments at that time (unless it's an appointment for ME). When I get up in the morning, I get dressed in my gym clothes, take my kids to school and head straight to the gym.

My workday starts a little later than some people would choose, but I tend to stay up pretty late (often working at night) and enjoy starting my day this way. Without a doubt it sets me in good stead for the day! This has become almost non-negotiable for me.

The times when I have scheduled things and am unable to work out in the morning, I start feeling resentful because I'm putting the needs of other people before my own (obviously there are times when I have to adjust my schedule, but for the most part, it's up to me). There have been a few times when I actually went to the gym earlier (like 5:30am) and then realized that no, that's not going to work. Maybe someday it will? But for now, I'm sticking with my routine.

My Bath: Debated a little with sharing this one – but, it is what it is! Without a doubt, I make time EVERY night for a nice long bubble bath! Regardless of having showered earlier in the day after the gym, I take time every night before I get in bed to have a nice long bath (my kids know what time they need to be in & out of the shower/bath so I have plenty of hot water!). I spend about an hour every night, reading and relaxing before I get in bed. Because what I do is so brain intensive it's imperative that I have a way to wind down and send a message to my brain that it's time to shut off! Sometimes I read non-fiction or business, but for the most part, it is a novel or a magazine (a non-business magazine).

Lastly, without a doubt, there are ways in which I incorporate quiet time, spirituality and writing into my life. I haven't created a definitive ritual here- but I know I'm getting closer. I've gone through different periods where I write affirmations, do some journaling or meditate (the meditation seems to be the hardest for me- maybe I need to stop 'working' so hard at it?). While I don't know what will 'stick' in this area, I do know that whatever the ritual may be, it's evolving.

So whatever rituals you have or don't have, know that deep down YOU know what's best for you.

About the Author: Kim Doyal, also known as 'The WordPress Chick' has been developing her online business full time for the past two and half years. Her love of WordPress evolved almost by accident. With a desire to build her own online marketing /information business she needed to find a way to get her websites up and running without having to constantly depend on other people.

Fast forward a couple years and Kim has surpassed her full time income with her "WordPress Chick" site, a video marketing continuity program and now, 'Women in Business 2.0, The Movie". A bit of an information junkie, Kim was always fascinated by individual stories of people who had overcome challenges and pursued their dreams. The Internet was no different. Visit Kim online at www.TheWPchick.com or www.WomenInBusinessTheMovie.com

Building Wealth from the Inside Out with Affirmations

LINDA P. JONES

O ne of the rituals I've used myself and with my clients, that has been proven to provide astounding results, is using affirmations. Even though affirmations are not new, many people don't use them or know how to use them effectively. Using affirmations is life changing, and I don't say that lightly. I've experienced incredible positive changes and my clients have been known to call me, crying with tears of joy, with how much they have changed their lives for the better. Do I have your attention?

Affirmations are statements you'd like to come true. They're not really a "wish" because wishes are something you just hope for, but don't do anything to cause them to come true. Affirmations are different because they actually re-program your subconscious. We have all heard that "your subconscious is in charge of your reality", but the funny thing is, because it's "sub" conscious, we're not consciously aware of what's in our subconscious! Are you still with me? We want to believe our subconscious is logical and might hope everything in it is all good, but the reality is, it's usually far from that.

What happens is emotional and/or repetitive thoughts and beliefs begin to go into our subconscious, beginning in our childhood, like our parents' beliefs about money, our experiences, TV and movies, songs, church rituals, etc. Different ideas get into our subconscious and we don't even know they are in there. It's like you're flying on a plane, an otherwise empty 747, you're in coach, and in the cockpit flying the plane is a 3 year old (your subconscious). It's like a 3 year old because it acts very primal. What you are doing when you create affirmations is putting a mature pilot in the cockpit and programming the plane's GPS to go where you want it to go!

Subconscious beliefs are not hard to change, it's just a matter of being deliberate with the beliefs you want and providing enough repetition.

Here's an easy way to use affirmations to change your subconscious beliefs:

First, think of 5-one sentence statements, in present tense, you would like to be true. Then think of five sentences that are already true. Now write them down, alternating one affirmation and one already true statement.

It looks like this:

Money is coming to me easily and effortlessly. (affirmation)

My name is Linda. (true)

I have the most amazing life and it's getting better every day. (affirmation)

My dog's name is Bailey. (true)

I love to exercise and am in great shape. (definitely an affirmation!)

I have blonde hair. (true)

I eat the most nutritious food every day for my ideal weight of _____. (affirmation)

I have two sisters. (true)

I feel happy, joyous, and incredibly grateful for my life and family every day. (affirmation)

I am the youngest child. (true)

Suggestions for the entrepreneur:

I have (number) _____ new clients this month at (amount) $ _____ each. (affirmation)

I live in Rancho Mirage. (true)

I make (dollar amount) $_____ in (month) _____. (affirmation)

I have a silver car. (true)

I love speaking on stage and am in great demand. (affirmation)

I have two brothers.

Clients are lining up to work with me and pay me my full price of $_____. (affirmation)

I live in California. (true)

I feel confident when asking for money for my services. (affirmation)

Now make up your own!

Think about different areas of your life you'd like to improve such as personal, physical, spiritual, lifestyle, money, and business. You can create several affirmations for each area, or just address the areas you feel strongest about improving.

Then, read them twice a day, morning and night is best, for 30 days in a row. Your brain will create a new pathway and start believing your affirmations. You'll notice it's no longer a stretch to believe them, you really DO believe them! They'll be in your subconscious directing you. Soon, they will outwardly begin coming true in your life. Try them. They work!

It's also a good idea, as long as you're creating what you want you life to be like, to include a vision statement of the life you'd like. A vision statement is how your "dream life" would be if you could create it (you do). Take an hour and go to a quiet place, take out a journal, and write the vision you see for your life and your family.

Begin writing your plan. It should include the vision of your life in 3 years. Let your thoughts flood out without any judgment. Don't give any thought of HOW you are going to accomplish anything that you write down. Write it without being reasonable! This is total fantasy. I want you to dream big. I want you to ask for a lot. It is only on paper and there's no commitment required on your part. None whatsoever. Don't think about HOW it will happen or be achieved. This is only the WHAT.

Write this in the way you would answer if I asked you, "What's your perfect day like?" Maybe you said, my best friend and I go to the beach, we are sitting at the Ritz Carlton, we go to the spa and indulge in all those services. Then my partner I have a romantic dinner, we take a walk on the beach holding hands, and we enjoy the beautiful sunset, etc. It is a dream without a commitment. Write it down. After you have written your statement, date it 3 years into the future. Again, there is no commitment.

Now, for your business specifically, you can write the perfect day with perfect clients. For this you are also going to include numbers. Some questions to ask might be: How much money are you making a month in your dream business? How much revenue does your dream business generate annually? And the one I like the most is, who do you have to "be" to deliver the service at the level you want?

Let me illustrate that. Let's say you want to speak in Madison Square Garden. You have a message that's so big you want to share it with the world, and a dream of yours is to speak in Madison Square Garden. Now, should you spend your time focusing on things like how to become a good speaker, what the content of your speech is, where you should stand on the stage, how you should gesture, how to look at the cameras? No! Work on who the person is you have to become to be comfortable speaking at Madison Square Garden! What are the things you have to believe about yourself to become that person who speaks at Madison Square Garden?

Let me give you another example. I recently was doing some work on the radio and had to go into a studio to record some radio spots. I had never been in a recording studio before and I was a little nervous about what to do. But I worked on my mindset and gave myself the right messages and the right way to be thinking about who I needed to be to deliver those messages.

In preparation, I wrote down seven short paragraphs or messages I wanted to get across on the radio. They weren't perfect. I didn't stress over each word. I just wrote out seven paragraphs. I went to the recording studio and the person who was going to be recording with me asked me, "What do you want to record?" I said, "I have written out some messages". I read him each one. He said ok, "I'll make up a question for each of your paragraphs and you answer what you wrote." I said alright. I put down my notes and we stood facing each other at the microphone. He asked me the question and I gave the answer. It went beautifully. And he said to me "This is going so well, have you done this before?" I said, "no". Almost every take went perfectly. He said "This is amazing."

I was so thrilled, because it wasn't that I had memorized every single word I was going to say and really fretted over it, or how I was going to deliver it and tried to control everything. No! What I had done for weeks in preparation was focus on who I needed to be and what my subconscious needed to feel about myself and believe about myself to be the person to deliver that message on the radio. It made all the difference because my subconscious was ready! I knew my material. I didn't need to memorize it. What I needed to do was give myself the instruction to be the right person to deliver the message!

By using affirmations about who I needed to be, I was creating my ideal life right before my eyes. The two go hand in hand and are very powerful. Suspend your disbelief and begin writing your affirmations and your vision statement now. You can thank me later!

About the Author: Linda P. Jones is a "Wealth Advocate" and her mission in life is to bring more wealth to the world and to show others the roadmap to financial freedom. She is CEO and founder of the Global Institute of Wealth for Women (GIWW), where women entrepreneurs learn about money and finance in an easy and fun way.

While in her late 20 s, she identified an 8 step process, "The 8 Steps to Wealth", she put into practice and it made her a millionaire at age 38. At 39, she made $1 million in one year. Life was lovely, until seven years later when tragedy struck, and her husband died suddenly from a brain aneurysm. She felt the calling to her life's purpose which is to share "The 8 Steps to Wealth" with the world. Get your free wealth building tools at: www.GlobalInstituteofWealthforWomen.com

5 Ways to Guarantee Success, Personally, Professionally and Spiritually

LISA MANYON

W hen asked how I've achieved all that I have I'm often mystified by the question. To me setting a goal and achieving it is as natural as breathing (although the outcome isn't always what I originally expect).

Success is relative. Let me explain. I don't really believe I am more successful than anyone else. I've reached a level of success that I've strived for because it's what I want. What I want and what you want may be two completely different things and that's OK. You should never let anyone but you determine your success, or failure for that matter. Plus, I believe success is ever evolving. What I want today may not be what I want tomorrow and I think that is part of the beauty of life. The most important thing is to enjoy life and do what you can to share your gifts with the world.

So, how do I achieve the success that I have? In my mind, there are five core foundations to success.

1. Self care is an essential piece of the success puzzle.

You may have heard the saying "it all begins within" and to me that means it all begins with taking the best care possible of me (or in your case, you). This is yet another ever-evolving process and it takes the form of healthy diet, exercise and learning about moderation. Simply put, I do the best that I can because I'm the only one who can truly take care of me. If I don't start there I couldn't possibly take care of or be fully present for anyone else.

Being your best self is another reason self care is vital. I can already hear many of the "yeah but" comments and they may seem valid to you. It's sometimes difficult to find the time we need for self care and at the same time it's essential. I realize you may think it's easier for me to do because, it's true, I am not a mom or a wife and so it may seem like a breeze for me to indulge in self care but it's truly not an indulgence – it's necessary. While I may not wear all the hats you do, I have other responsibilities too and sometimes it's a struggle to carve our self care time. Begin taking better care of yourself and you'll see a noticeable difference in all areas of your life.

My best tip for self care: Make it a part of your routine. Schedule "you" time and stick to it just like you do your other priorities and appointments.

2. Professional growth is a must if you want to achieve your goals.

Think about this: People are generally willing to invest as much in you as you are willing to invest in yourself. This means if you are not regularly learning and growing to be of the best service possible, people will notice and your success will be impacted. If your main objection to investing in you has been financial it's time to get a handle on that. First shift the way you think about the 'cost' of training, programs and education. This is vital. Anything that you invest in to better yourself is just that, an investment -- not an expense.

Instead of thinking about how much something might cost I think about how it will help me grow and succeed. Admittedly this drives my accountant crazy but it's paid off in the end even if it didn't seem like it might at first. Instead of coming up with a million excuses as to why you cannot do something come up with as many solutions as possible to make it happen. I'm a firm believer that where there is a will there is a way.

My best tip for professional growth: Weigh your options carefully and continually invest in programs where you'll find the best return on investment personally, professionally and spiritually.

3. Spiritual growth will help you move forward no matter where you are.

Never fear, this is not going to be a mini sermon. In fact, I honor your beliefs no matter what they are. I personally believe there is something much bigger than all of us and I like to learn about the different religious and spiritual practices throughout the world.

Exposing yourself to different beliefs is essential to growing as a person. It's also very helpful to know there is a force much bigger than any of us and sometimes it's important to "let go and let God" (or insert the deity of your choice here).

I've discovered that if I'm focusing too much on the "how" it's time to let go and give universal laws some time to start working for me. Spiritual growth takes many forms and it's up to you to discover what works best for you and truly feeds your soul.

My best tip for spiritual growth: Don't be afraid to pray. Sometimes even that small act can make a huge difference. If you're not comfortable praying, try meditation.

4. Personal growth is a never ending journey – embrace it and enjoy the ride to success.

It's perfectly okay to be set in your ways to a certain degree. I also understand that your life is full of demands and you may sometimes feel lost in all of your responsibilities and obligations. At the same time approaching life and experiences with an open mind can open new opportunities.

My goal is to never pass up a chance to learn something new or interesting. I'm way beyond the amassing "stuff" stage and I want everything I do to be a rich experience that creates the treasure of beautiful memories. The best way to do this is to discover what you love to do and do it. Live your "bucket" list now so you don't live with regret later. At the very least discover what brings you joy and do it – it could even be very simple things like reading, hiking, cooking, golfing, joining a book club or wine tasting.

One of my favorite sayings is "Never resist a temporary inconvenience if it results in a permanent improvement."

My best tip for personal growth: Just do it. Make it a priority to engage in an activity that you've always wanted to explore but haven't found the time for. Make the time.

5. Celebrate your accomplishments with a Journal of Success.

Chronicling your successes may feel a bit uncomfortable at first especially for women. After all, society has programmed us to be humble and not to brag. But your journal of success is your own personal record of the incredible things you do each and every day. Accomplishments can be big or small. The only thing that matters is that you've done it and it's important to celebrate.

Find a beautiful notebook and fun pen and be sure to record each delicious accomplishment in your life. When I'm having an off day I flip through the pages of my success journal and am reminded of how far I've come and I'm reminded of triumphs both small and big. This also reminds me that I can do even more if I so choose.

My best tip for celebrating success: Try the success journal for a minimum of one week and see how it feels. You deserve it! Don't be shy or bashful. You are a remarkable person. Everything you do matters and it's important to give yourself credit.

Finally – be grateful for what is. Once you've embraced gratitude for what is you open the space for more to come into your life. And always remember your success depends on what you truly want, not what society dictates is "right" or anyone else says you should do. Be bold. Be Brave. Embrace success on your terms.

About the Author: Lisa Manyon is the President of Write On ~ Creative Writing Services, LLC., Professional Copywriter, Marketing Strategist and Published Author specializing in POWERFULLY communicating your marketing message to increase results. She is a master of matching your message to market in your authentic voice.

Manyon has a passion for helping people reach their individual goals. She helps transform dreams into manageable action steps with tangible results. Her passion for authentically sharing newsworthy messages has earned her recognition for press release and publicity results. You'll find Lisa online at www.WriteOnCreative.com

Relationships – The Heart and Soul of Your Business

MARY KAY MORGAN

Relationships are the heart and soul of your business. They are your business's most powerful growth and revenue accelerators. They also, I believe, make being in business truly a worthwhile experience. This chapter will identify your three most important business relationships, and they may surprise you.

In the old-school model of business, the business relationships most associated with success were the business owner's relationship with his or her clients/customers and his or her competitors. In a nutshell your client/customer was the person who were trying to get money from and your competitor was the one you were trying to keep money from! Not very warm and fuzzy!

The new-school model of business is quite different! While your relationship to your customer or client is still very important, the goal in no longer to squeeze as much money as you can from them any more! And "competitors" have evolved in many cases to become "strategic partners". However, neither your customers nor your strategic partners are you most important business relationships. Here are the three that I believe come first:

Essential Business Relationship #1: YOU!

Socrates' fundamental teaching was "Know thyself". Your life begins and ends with you. How well do you know yourself? What inspires you? Do you have conscious awareness of your core values? Do you know what you are here to do? Who and how do you want to be in this world when you grow up? These questions are answered when you know your core values and your soul's purpose.

Values and purpose are similar but not the same. Your values are the experiences you want to create just for you. Your values complete the sentence, "I'm happy when…" For example, some value freedom while others prefer structure. Some thrive under pressure and chaos while others want a quiet, orderly lifestyle. If you long to be home with your children yet choose to climb the corporate ladder because you can (or you don't realize you have options), you will be out of sync with your values! Your values are expressing how you are or want to be living your life.

Your purpose, on the other hand, is your point of service to the world. It is an active expression of your gifts in such a way that others benefit. You can be on purpose in any number of settings – a job, your activities within your community, or through a business. When you are on purpose you will feel the great sense of satisfaction that comes from knowing you are being of service. When you sync your values with your purpose, true magic happens in your life!

Most people never give a second thought to what they value or to their purpose in life. They don't know why they want – or think they want - what they want. If you asked a typical response would be something like, "I don't know. That's just me.", or "That's just how I was raised. I can't change it." But is that true? How can a person tell when a choice is from conditioning rather than from the authentic values and call to purpose of their very own soul?

We begin to be conditioned as soon as we are born, and many experts believe conditioning begins even before birth. Regardless of exactly when, it is clear that we had very little say in the matter! The answer is a conditioned choice will drain your energy and leave an empty feeling inside.

Imagine the young woman who wants to be a dancer but chooses law school because everyone always told her she will "be a great lawyer like her mom one day", or the young man who desperately wants to travel the world but instead works the family retail business because everyone expects him to do so. In each case, they may plug along for a while, perhaps an entire lifetime, but instead of feeling filled up by their work they will feel a nagging emptiness, a longing for more and a deep fatigue that cannot be slept away.

Being in conscious, aligned relationship with your values and your purpose is priority in creating a successful business. It allows you to know without question what is a "Hell yes!" and what is a firm "No" in your business. This clarity is also essential to creating successful affiliate and joint venture choices.

Teasing our authentic self from the conditioned self does not usually happen overnight. It involves a willingness to really feel into whether something is serving you (hint: if something serves your soul it will raise your energy level) or if you are making choices based on the values of another (depletes your energy).

The essential steps to unraveling self from other are:

1. Meditation – the consistent practice of quieting the mind and going within is fundamental to beginning and continuing to hear your authentic inner voice

2. Get Out of Your Box – if you feel drawn to something, take it for a test drive. I first answered my inner call to be an entrepreneur not by quitting my job and investing all my savings on "my dream" but by joining a network marketing

company. It was the perfect stepping stone to how I express as an entrepreneur today.

3. Accept that you are a work in progress – as my yoga teacher says, "There's no pot of gold at the end of the pose!" Enjoy the process of unfolding to your truth rather than trying to "figure it all out" in a weekend

4. Enlist the assistance of a professional mirror – aka: a coach! A great coach creates the opportunity for you to see yourself more clearly. They are indispensible to the process!

Essential Business Relationship #2: Your Personal Relationships

In the old-school model of business previously mentioned, the last relationships a business owner considered as important to his or her business success were the personal ones – spouses, partners, children, family, friends - all took a back seat to the demands of the business.

In the new-school model, rare is the entrepreneur who isn't seeking "whole life" success, and "whole life" includes experiencing the flow life with and through the people we love and care about! Humans are by nature "pack animals". We must be in positive energy exchange with our family and friends for optimum, whole-life fulfillment – physical, mental, emotional and spiritual. A baby who has every physical need met but no love, no meaningful emotional exchange with another, will die. As adults we are really just big babies!

Our personal relationships not only make life worth living, they allow us to be fully alive and show up the best we can be. Think about it, are you more productive when your personal relationships are in flow or after you've had a fight with your spouse, best friend or child?

Who are the five most important people in your life? How much time are you spending with them, being present to them, relating to them? Do you need to set better boundaries for yourself so that you can be present to your business when it calls and to your personal relationships when it is their time?

As a single-mom and business owner, I came to the realization (after quite a bit of struggle) that there was no way I could create "balance" between my children and my business. Attempting to do so always left one a little short of the other like a bad seesaw. It was only when I made the decision to be fully present to work during work time and fully present to my children during their time that my experience and my business began to shift. I had to set a boundary in order for this to happen and the boundary I had to set was for myself! Commit to taking that time to be present your personal relationships. Your business will thank you for it.

Essential Business Relationship #3 – Your Business

How well do you know your business? How often to you give it the focus and intentional attention it deserves. Now, I realize that you are probably thinking, "I work in my business everyday!", and perhaps that is the problem. When you are working, working, working, in your business you are not working on and with your business.

Every creation is an energetic entity so in a very real way you are in relationship with your business. When was the last time you paused to be conscious and aware of this business you have created? How do you feel about your business? Are you excited and joyful when you think about your business or disappointed and perhaps resentful?

You cannot create abundance from a foundation of negative energy. If you are in relationship with your business from a negative place, this is no time for denial or a glaze of "positive thinking". If your business is not bringing a sense of happiness and joy, it's imperative that you take the time to find out what is really going on between you two. Come to recognition of the truth and change what needs changing!

A solution to reigniting the flame of passion for your business is very similar to how you might reignite the flames of passion for a lover – get away for a couple of days just the two of you! Or in the case of your business, with a facilitator who can assist you in getting your original "why" back on track and finding a multitude of new reasons to keep saying yes to this incredible being called your business. Cozy up with some flip charts and several vibrantly colored Sharpies® and you'll be feeling all hot to go again in no time!

You, your significant others and your business – one, two and three on my list of most important business relationships for success!

About the Author: Mary Kay Morgan, MS is founder of Affiliate Wealth Partners.com the only affiliate and joint venture networking and "how to" resource devoted exclusively to increasing the market visibility and the sales revenue of conscious businesses through the development of aligned, authentic and effective affiliate and joint venture relationships.

Mary Kay is the industry's leading expert at increasing your "business-relationship" IQ and EQ so that you can create long-term business relationships that are both personally rewarding and profitable.

Mary Kay is here today to identify and share with you how to avoid the most common mistakes made by heart-centered entrepreneurs in the two most common vehicles for relationship marketing – affiliates and joint ventures. www.AffiliateWealthPartners.com

Creating Your Day By Design: A Daily Grand Ritual for Massive Success

NACHHI RANDHAWA

It has been said that beyond ideas of wrongdoing and rightdoing, there is a field. To me, that field of doing right in living our dreams and creating daily success begins with what has become known to me as my '**Daily Grand Ritual to Massive Success**.' Starting the day right and following key rituals that I've set up for myself has truly become my biggest and quietest secret to success.

Having grown up as a night owl instead of the early bird that I longed to be and that I am now, I've tried a myriad of ideas between wrongdoing and rightdoing. To say the least, the way you set up your day can have a profound effect on the success you create, both personally and professionally.

We all have certain rituals that we follow daily. In its most simplistic form, a ritual is basically just a routine you become accustomed to. For example, waking up a certain time, having breakfast at a set time, going to work at a planned time, and having dinner at the same time each evening. These are all rituals. We may not be aware of them and not think of them as rituals because they have become a part of us and our daily living that we often do those things unconsciously and on auto-pilot.

When I started gaining a deep interest in my desire to go from the unconscious realm to a conscious world of possibilities, the first and biggest change I made was in creating a daily ritual, and an early morning ritual at that with the hopes of taking my biological clock to a space of quiet thought and creation time. It still amazes me how out of our deepest and greatest needs to find balance and focus, often the most beautiful yet powerful rituals are birthed.

Here are my daily rituals for creation, magic, and success:

1. Starting my day with an early morning walk. This gives me time to start afresh another beautiful day and to voice my gratitude to the divine and to find answers during this quiet, reflective walk or jog.

2. Meditating in a beautifully created personal home sanctuary. As I sit down to meditate, I first pull out my journal and write any questions or thoughts I'd like divine answers to. This helps me create the focus for my morning meditation, which I've come to really know as a meeting with my highest self.

3. Enjoying a warm cup of morning tea while sitting with my journal and writing any answers or ideas that came from my meditation. I then pull out one of the magical index cards that I store in my journal and on top of the card I write: "Today's Grand FOCUS for Productive and Yummy Results." Then I relax, take a few deep breaths, and think for a minute of three things that if completed that day, I will feel fantastic about my day and be able to enjoy a beautiful evening with my family, knowing that my day has been wildly productive and massively successful. Next, I number and write these

three things on the card. This card has come to be known as my Daily Grand FOCUS Intention Card and is my biggest secret to productivity and meeting my daily goals.

4. Taking my Focus Intention Card and placing it on the corner of my desk with a beautiful crystal rock to hold the card in place and to draw my focus to it throughout the day. On the other corner of my desk, I light a candle and then take a minute to close my eyes and set my intentions for completing the three tasks on my focus card. As I sit down to write or work on my marketing or to lead a teleclass, my focus card keeps me visually reminded of my objectives for the day and keeps me turned away from distractions. Like in meditation, we often turn back to the breath when outside thoughts start creeping in. My focus card is a special and gentle reminder to turn back to the task at hand instead of getting sidetracked by the multitudes of other things vying for my attention.

5. Celebrating the completion of another amazing day and completion of my three tasks that I wrote on my focus intention card! The remainder of my daily ritual is to close the day with a quick review of what I've completed and then enjoy the evening with my family and close for the night with a little inspirational reading, a heart full of gratitude, and a nightly prayer.

Having created a daily ritual has become the guiding light for the success and growth of my business. It's allowed me to build a flourishing practice by coming in tune with what I need to create on any given day. More than anything, the start of my day allows me to fully wake up and to breathe in the beauty of life and to voice all that I am grateful for. The tuning in within the self is incredibly powerful in both creating a day by design and in awakening my inner voice, the voice that tells me that all is okay and that this new day is filled with infinite possibilities.

A few tips for creating your own daily routine would be to grab a journal, take some quiet time, light a candle, and answer these questions in your journal:

1. What one thing can you do each morning to jumpstart your day and create the energy you need for a magical and productive day ahead? For me, that idea is to start my morning with a quiet, reflective walk or jog. What one thing can you do?

2. What can you do to create some "think time" each morning to plan for a successful day? For me, it's meditation and then writing in my journal and creating my daily focus while slowly sipping some tea. What can you do to create your own think time each morning?

3. What three things can you do today to really feel fantastic about your day if they got completed? Listing three things has worked like magic for me to keep it manageable and to not be sidetracked by the hundreds of things that can get me distracted if I don't create the focus for what I need to do. What is doable for you each day? List those items on a FOCUS card and place it somewhere prominent in your work area so that it literally becomes your focus point whenever distractions surface. Allow this focus card to pull you back into the groove of that which is most important at the moment. Creating this focused intent and blocking out this time daily just for you will create magic in your day and business.

Having a daily routine can have a profound effect on your daily life and that of your business. How often do you keep mentally reminding yourself of all that needs to be done or scrolling back through your long to-do list? And at the end of the day, you wonder where the time went. I have often wondered that myself and after countless days and hours lost of finding the perfect remedy to really create my day by design and to dance with the flow of what needs to be done at any given moment, I found it best to create a scheduled ritual that creates for a magical and successful day.

Being a business owner and owning your own schedule is no easy task when you are no longer confined to the schedule of a daily work day. I chose to find a path that works for me and I must say that having a daily ritual is truly magic. It allows me to manage my time and to get my work done within my scheduled office hours. It allows me to have some quiet "me time" to think and reflect. It allows me to have treasured family time where I am fully present.

While it's very important to create focus and achieve success on a daily basis, it's equally important to fill your energy on a daily basis to continuously function at a high vibration and to take your life's deepest dreams and longings from your mental reality to the physical realm. So in addition to your daily ritual, think about what you can do to fill your energy levels and keep the momentum going.

For me, that is a nightly routine of doing a little inspirational reading and journaling. I have at least one inspirational book on my nightstand at all times. Take a little time today and go through your favorite books. Try some audio books if you are on the road a lot. Download your favorite teleclasses onto your iPod and listen while out walking and connecting with nature. Create a personal home sanctuary and make it your special place to meditate, write, and tune within to your highest self.

You were born to create and to shine a powerful light in the world. That world starts with you and your daily practice of honoring yourself by creating soul-satisfying rituals in attainment of your grandest dreams and in making a difference. Start today and allow yourself to walk into your rituals, open up to your creativity, and let your dreams take root and take you to levels beyond and even more powerful than your imagination. That's what happens when we take the time each day to nurture our souls, intently plan our day, execute our grand plans, and breathe in total and complete success.

May your days be massively productive and may you be wildly successful!

About the Author: *Nachhi is an author, speaker, certified spiritual and professional coach, Heal Your Life® Teacher, 1Hour Mastermind Director, founder and owner of Grand Life Solutions, and the proud mother of two beautiful children. Nachhi inspires and supports heart-centered individuals and business leaders in finding their vision, mastering their life, and building their dreams. Visit Nachhi at www. GrandLifeSolutions.com*

A Simple System (and a Dirty Little Secret) for Completing Monster Projects

NIKA STEWART

Many people are drawn to entrepreneurship because of the delicious freedom and flexibility it provides. As business owners, we have complete control over the direction of our companies, the intensity of our schedules, the projects we pursue, how much work we do, and the amount of success we achieve.

But there is also another kind of freedom that is not as tasty: Entrepreneurs have the freedom to procrastinate; to put projects off indefinitely; to miss self-imposed deadlines. And what's the big deal? After all, we are our own bosses – accountable to no one but ourselves. As entrepreneurs, we have the flexibility to adjust our schedules, reprioritize tasks, and extend deadlines – even on the most critical projects.

And that's the problem. While entrepreneurism boasts countless advantages over working for someone else's company, **one of its most debilitating drawbacks is its lack of inherent accountability.**

191

For employees, accountability is a core requirement of the job. When your boss sets a deadline for a project, she expects it to be completed by that date. Your job is to manage your time appropriately to deliver the project on time. If personal or family situations arise, or if you're just too tired to finish, you don't have the option to put the project off until the next day. And while entrepreneurs enjoy the luxury of procrastination, they also suffer the curse of its consequences.

So how do business owners acquire the benefits of accountability while still enjoying the flexibility of being self-employed?

When I first became a Laptop Mom in 2005, I occasionally succumbed to the temptations of postponing deadlines. When facing an enormous workload and an impossible schedule – because of family and work commitments – it was easy to justify closing my computer and putting projects off until the next day (or week, or year!). The problem is that if an idea sits around too long before being implemented, it tends to lose its steam and sometimes never makes it back on the front burner.

After having several great ideas fall by the wayside, I created a basic system and a powerful little secret that provides me with the accountability I want along with the flexibility I need. The system is basic and helpful, but the extra secret ingredient is foolproof.

Here is my system and my DLS (Dirty Little Secret):

In the first place, planning is essential. I have come to learn that there is a limit to the amount of projects that can be accomplished at any given time. Once my plate is full, I need to focus on completing ongoing projects before I take on new ones. If not, my existing projects suffer, and I end up pushing them to the back burner indefinitely. *Finish what you've started before beginning something new.*

Set deadlines and keep them. When beginning a project, it must be reverse engineered starting from the completion date. Create a realistic timeline with concrete goals and milestones. Keep on pace and resolve obstacles to be sure to meet your ultimate deadline. Have you fallen behind on the project? Creating a little backlog every day adds up to major delays by the end of the project. So as soon as you find yourself falling behind, catch up! Sometimes that means burning the midnight oil or hiring a babysitter for an extra few hours. Just because you are self-employed and can put work off until the next day, doesn't mean you should. *Follow the schedule as if you were accountable to a boss.*

Once you have committed to a project, publicize it heavily. Make sure your friends, family, customers, and prospects are aware of your project. Announcing it publicly provides accountability by adding external pressure to meeting your goal. Now you have something at stake. A missed deadline will make you red-faced at best, and at worst can portray you as unreliable and unprofessional. *Let the world know about it.*

Understand what the end result means to your business and your life. Sometimes we lose sight of the "why" behind the "what." Keep reminding yourself how your business will benefit once you have fully implemented the project. Put it on your bulletin board, create note cards, send yourself reminders – anything you need to keep the motivation going until the project is done.

The sense of accomplishment you feel at the end of a challenging project almost always outweighs the burden of completing it. (Launching a new product is kind of like childbirth. Just go with me on this one... Yes, there is some pain. Yes, it can be exhausting. But once it's over, all you think about is the beautiful baby you've created. You forget about the pain, and you focus on the joy that comes from it.) *Never lose sight of the end result.*

So there's the basic system. Will it help you to complete your projects? Absolutely. But let's face it: **It is anything but foolproof.** Even if you select and plan your projects, set your deadlines, tell everyone about your project, and focus on what the project's completion will mean to you and your life, there is certainly no guarantee that you will finish your project – on time or otherwise. And the reason for this is that **the consequences for not finishing are still not all that bad.** What's the worst that will happen if you do not finish? You'll fall a little behind? Your friends will tease you about not finishing what you started? You won't reap the reward you desire? Big deal! These consequences – although damaging – are certainly not enough to guarantee that you finish your project on time. What we need is a surefire, 100% guaranteed effective method to be sure that we reach our goals. And that's where my Dirty Little Secret comes in.

My Dirty Little Secret (DLS)

So what is my method for guaranteeing that my project is completed on time? It's this: Whenever I decide to create a new product or program, I sell it first. Yes, you read it correctly. I announce the launch date and start offering the program – even before it is created!

Utter lunacy, you say? It's actually not as crazy as it seems.

Creating the sales page is very similar to writing the outline of the product or program. It is an excellent first step. Once the outline/sales page is created, I have a roadmap for completing the product. And now that the sales page is live and customer orders start coming in, I have a deadline that can NOT be broken. Because If I miss this deadline, there is a lot more at stake than being teased by my friends. I will have to return money. And because I am excellent at marketing my products, there would be a LOT of money I would have to return! :)

With this type of motivation, finishing my project on time is guaranteed.

Creating a product is an exciting process, and with pre-order sales coming in, I know that I will finish on time, as promised.

Now that you know my Dirty Little Secret, try it yourself! You will see how well it works.

About the Author: Nika Stewart is a lifestyle entrepreneur: A professional who has seamlessly integrated her career into her life.

After building a successful career as an award-winning designer, Nika created a new business so she could spend quality time with her family. She leveraged her knowledge and developed information products that teach designers to build profitable businesses.

Nika discovered that other moms were also searching for businesses they could run from home, allowing the flexibility to take care of family priorities. So Nika launched www.LaptopMom.com to show moms how to create passive income and build a successful business... during naptime!

Intention to Action: The Essence of Success Rituals

PATRICA SELMO

As an interfaith - interspiritual teacher and healer I am very aware of the importance of ritual. **Ritual can help us see ourselves as the connection between heaven and earth – it brings the spiritual to the mundane.**

The word "Ritual" actually comes from an Indo-European root word, which means "to Fit together"; this is actually an act of joining the spiritual world with the physical world. Ritual is a path to the Divine.

What makes something a ritual as opposed to just a habit? INTENTION!!! There are two parts to every ritual: Intention and the Action ("Heart" and "Hand"). The intention is the purpose of the ritual – it is what we hope to accomplish by performing it. By putting our **intentions into action**, we create a space in which we are fully present in the moment – we are in a state of MINDFULNESS. The ego dissolves and we are connected with Source.

One of my purposes is to be always in connection with the Divine and to help others to do the same. **When you are "con-**

nected", things flow so much more smoothly, decisions are easier and conflicts are eased.

In the daily rush, it is easy to just quickly move from one task to the next – blindly going through life and not finding meaning in any of it. But ritual can help us come back to ourselves…to make that connection with our Source and to be sure we are focused and on the right track. What could be better than that?

I think many of us go into business for ourselves because we want more meaning in our lives and in our work. But, what is meaning exactly? I would venture to say that it is that spiritual, sacred essence that can so easily get brushed aside when we are always in a hurry. Ritual can take you back there in an instant – into a focused state where we can notice where we are and intend what we want.

The way to live with the Divine as your business partner is to transform everyday events into sacred moments. Any action can become a ritual by focusing intent on it. Anything from brushing your teeth or writing an email can become a sacred act.

My recommended success ritual is to connect with the Divine every day throughout the day. This is not so much one ritual, but many that can be clumped under the umbrella of "Divine Connection". These small rituals throughout the day are what make me successful. And I know immediately when I haven't been keeping up my daily sacred rituals to connect, because I become agitated and anxious more easily, things don't flow as smoothly, and the river of abundance appears to be "dammed-up"!

So, how do you make this Divine Connection throughout the day?

The first step is to create a Sacred Space – this could be an altar, a corner of a room where you can pray or meditate or even at your desk…you could also do all three of these! The idea is that you have a place that you can return to throughout the day to stop, pull away from your worldly affairs and focus on the affairs of the heart or spirit. As Joseph Campbell so eloquently puts it:

"This is a place
where you can simply experience
and bring forth what you are and what you
might be. This is the place of creative
incubation. At first you might find that
nothing happens there.
But if you have a sacred place and use it,
Something eventually will happen...Your
Sacred space is where
You find yourself again and again."

Fill this space with objects that have meaning to you, photos of loved ones, a rock or feather from nature, sacred texts, copies of favorite poems, incense, etc. Place there anything that is meaningful to you and fills you with peace. As you use this space more and more it will become filled with the sacred energy of your prayers and meditations.

The Second step is to schedule time. Make this a part of your daily activities. Schedule some of these practices at natural breaks in your day such as meals, waking up and going to sleep. Others, such as the mid-day prayers I suggest should be scheduled ahead of time and an alarm set to remind you to stop and pray or meditate at those times. During these times of recharging, make sure your phone is off and any email or other alarms are off. Make sure no one will interrupt you during this time. You should not be multi-tasking at all, but taking a 5-minute break to sit with your Source.

General Guidelines

Some ideas to get you going on your appointment with Source and to listen to that inner voice are:

- Make time throughout the day

- Stop work at 5 PM – step away from the computer; clear your desk and get out what you need for the next day

- Mark transitions through mini-rituals

  - End of day

  - Start of day

  - Meals

  - Etc.

- Do not multi-task – stay in the moment, focused on your intention

- When changing tasks, do something creative – dance, sing, write, paint. For example, when changing from answering emails to writing a blog post, get up and color on a pad with some crayons, or put on some music and dance around your office.

Remember that the intention behind ritual is to develop and maintain a habit of mindfulness. Focus on the one thing you are doing each and every moment of the day – this will keep you in the present moment where you can fully open up to that still, small voice within.

Sample Day

So, a typical day might look something like the following:

7 AM   *Wake-up*

Before arising, lay in bed and imagine your day, think of all your scheduled activities and tasks. Imagine yourself going through each of these activities and completing them with ease and joy. Imagine all your tasks turning out in the perfect way for you. Give thanks for this new day!

7:15 AM   Shower

As the warm water is flowing over you, focus on the intention that all negativity is being washed away; that any past mistakes or regrets are flowing down the drain – you are beginning a new day, full of promise.

7:30 AM   Breakfast

Say a short blessing of gratitude over your food – imagine all the plants, animals, and people that were instrumental in getting it to your plate; ask that it fulfill and nourish you

8 AM   Begin Work

Sit down at your desk – Light a candle and state a blessing of intention to be filled with Grace toady and that all your acts are divinely-guided.

10 AM   Mid-morning – Prayer/meditation break

Set an alarm to make sure you stop. Go to your sacred space and get silent. Focus on your heart and release any tension or negativity that has built up there. Again give thanks and ask for guidance.

12 PM   Lunch

Blessing over food (as done at breakfast); after lunch, play a lively song and dance to it. This will revitalize you and get you ready for the rest of the day. As you are moving your body, notice how it feels, give thanks that you are able to move!

2 PM   Mid-afternoon – Prayer/meditation

Same as mid-morning break

5 PM   End of business day

Clean off your desk; review the tasks and appointments for the next day and place any client files or other items you need for the next day neatly on your clean desk – ready for you in the morning. Blow out the candle if it is still it.

5:15   Transition/recharge time

Take 15 minutes or so to transition back into your personal life. This can be done with a short prayer in your sacred space, a short meditation. The meditation could be as simple as closing your eyes and focusing on your breath for 15 minutes. Follow this (or do it at the same time) with Savasana. This is the yoga pose in which you lie on your back completely relaxed and let all tension flow out of you. You will find this leaves you refreshed for the rest of the evening.

6 PM   Dinner – blessing/prayer

Walk after dinner – be in nature. Nature is a simple and beautiful way to reconnect with the Divine – even in a city, you can walk and notice the sky, birds, or any other signs of nature around you.

10 PM   Prayer before bed

Review your day and look at where you could have improved and what you did well. Write down your accomplishments in your journal. Then list five things you are grateful for. When that is complete, write a letter to God with any concerns or issues you are having. You can then either listen for a response and write it down or ask to dream about it that night. Write down your dream in the morning.

Obviously your schedule may differ slightly. Perhaps you have children to take care of or odd working hours. This is really just to give you an idea and perhaps get your creative juices flowing as to how you can incorporate some of these rituals into your personal schedule.

I think that once you start incorporating moments of connection with the Divine into your day, you will find more and more ways to make every moment sacred. When you walk in sacred space every day, you will find success and abundance and inner peace in magnitudes unheard of in your prior life. I wish you all success and deep love – blessings.

About the Author: Patricia Selmo is a former Aerospace Engineer turned Interfaith Minister, Life Coach and Energy Healer. She has over 20 years of experience facilitating, coaching and managing professionals in the corporate environment. She now uses a unique combination of Spiritual Counseling, Ancient Wisdom (or Astrology) and Modern Science (Quantum Physics) to help people who are stuck or wanting more out of life to align with their soul purpose, connect with their Source and live an abundant life – on their own terms

You can get to know Patricia by reading her blog at www. TheBlissfulSoul. com

Life and Business by Design

RANDI PIERCE

There is massive power in creating a life and business that is in alignment with your authentic self. It's where purpose, passion and profit merge; where clients are irresistibly attracted to you; where prospects go from Sold to Souled™; and success feels effortless. This is the place where fear dissolves and confidence rules; where scarcity is replaced by abundance.

This is a **Life - And Business - By Design**. And creating it is much easier than you think.

Let me back up for just a moment…

From a very young age I had clear visions of how I wanted my life to be – and that vision was much different from what I had been taught about "real" life. I come from a solid familial line of laborers; generations of workers who, day in and day out, labored for decades - while hating every moment of it.

I was determined to live a different story...

I wasn't sure how that would be accomplished, so I essentially felt my way through it.

Right out of high school, I landed a job as a receptionist for a multi-billion dollar real estate company. Within a few months I was promoted to Administrative Assistant and would later go on to be promoted to Assistant Regional Marketing Director. I loved it – with the exception of the J-O-B part. I thrived on the high pressure and fast pace. I loved being surrounded by entrepreneurs who were, by initial accounts, abundant in all areas of their lives. They drove luxury cars, wore expensive suits, determined their own hours, and traveled the world....I wanted that.

But as the shiny-object syndrome wore off, the reality of their lives weren't perfect. They were stressed out, took client phone calls at 10 o'clock at night, worked weekends, and their personal relationships suffered from the demands of their careers.

Like many people, I had the skewed perception that the more money you made, the fewer problems you had; but that was hardly the case for the hundreds of entrepreneurs I worked with over the years.

I would go on to work with successful entrepreneurs in other industries, and saw the same story play out over and over. Put quite simply, 99% of the entrepreneurs I worked with were absolutely miserable. Sure, many of them were millionaires and multi-millionaires, but the cost of their success was obvious. As desperately as I wanted financial success, I wasn't willing to pay the price I had seen so many others pay. Honestly, I wanted more money, but did not want any more problems.

Given my experiences with entrepreneurs across several industries, it appeared that success seemed to be a double-edged sword. Yet, despite the obvious appearance, I had an unyielding gut feeling that it didn't have to be. I knew, deep down, that it was possible to live my life and build a successful business without having to sacrifice or struggle.

It would be almost two decades before I discovered the hidden formula.

That's where the ***Life ~ By Design Formula*™** comes in.

It's a system that helps you build your business from the inside out – a business that is designed, by you, to be in complete alignment with who you are.

This is the missing piece that most entrepreneurs don't even know exists…

They are running a business that is an endless struggle because it is not in alignment with who they really are…Not because they don't want a better way to do it – it's that they haven't been shown how to build a business differently.

Struggles in business can always be traced back to elements not in alignment with your authenticity, purpose or desires – every single time. It's fool-proof, replicable, and reliable.

Not only does the *Life ~ By Design Formula*™ remove elements that are the cause of struggle, it actually helps you achieve success (however you define it) faster and easier. When your life and business are in alignment with each other – and with who you really are – everything heads in the same direction, naturally supporting your authenticity, purpose and desires.

When everything is headed in the same direction, there is no longer a compartmentalization to life that causes you to split your focus between contrasting ideas. And this is exactly why the majority of the people on this planet struggle in multiple areas of their lives.

Anytime there is opposing energy, you will find struggle: You find joy in one area of your life, but dread another. You love your family, but hate your job. You love your career, but the time and energy it requires negatively affects your relationships.

It becomes an endless cycle of struggling between two opposing forces…

It IS possible to design your life and business in the exact way it works for you – without struggle – and in a way that attracts abundance. This is the magical factor of business that took me two decades to uncover!

The catch is that most entrepreneurs don't realize it's possible…

So how do you achieve flow, ease and abundance in your life and business? Here are 5 simple, yet powerful principles you can put into action immediately to start creating positive changes today:

Get Clear About What You Really Want

The most important thing in life is to be as clear as possible about what you want. The universe wants to provide the things you want more than you desire them, but it cannot deliver it when you are not clear.

> *TIP: Make a list of 10 to 20 things that you would like to see in your life right now. If you can imagine it, the way to achieve it already exists. Getting very clear about what you really want is the first step in creating it. I strongly suggest writing the list in pen in your own hand for the biggest results. Review the list often and update it as needed.*

Dump What Isn't Working

Please, please, please stop doing anything that is causing struggle. If your job is making you miserable – find another income source. If your clients are driving you crazy AND they're not paying you what you're worth – dump them. If your relationships are more of a burden than joy – explore the source of tension.

> *TIP: Remember, areas of struggles are symptoms of what is not in alignment with who you really are. Keep tweaking what isn't working until you find a way that it does work.*

Integrate What You Love To Do Into Your Business – Now!

This principle can easily get swept under the rug or put on the To Do Later list, but this is actually a vital key to creating more joy and more income. Anything that you love to do carries more value than you may initially be aware of – and should be integrated into your business immediately.

> *TIP: The things you love to do are often the things that carry the most value – and what you can charge the most for. (Hint, hint.)*

Think Outside the Box – Get Creative

There are millions of people across the globe who get paid to do what they love – and you can create the same reality in your own life. The way you've been taught to run your business is not the only way to run it. The more assertion you exhibit in designing your life and business, the more successful you will be. Creative power carries great universal support – and you are a creator. You have all the resources you need to create your life, and business, the way it works for you.

> *TIP: When designing products, programs and services, always start with what you want to do. From there, you can package it so it meets the needs of your clients. I predict we'll see great emphasis on creative business practices over the next decade – and I think you'll be surprised that the boundaries of business will almost be indistinguishable from personal time.*

There is Massive Power in Authenticity

Your greatest area of strength is in your authenticity. Don't try to compartmentalize your life from your business or vice versa. Nor should you confine your business practices because you're afraid what people might think. Design your business as an expression of your authentic self because, quite frankly, without authenticity you will not be able to attract your ideal clients. They won't be able to see you for who you really are if you're hiding out behind a façade.

> *TIP: The moment you allow your business to be an expression of your authentic self is the moment you go from looking for clients to them seeking you out. They will be instantly attracted to you — and eager to pay you what you're worth — because they will see the real you. When you are stepping up and stepping out into the world comfortable and confident in who you are, you'll have more clients and raving fans than you can count.*

This much I know: You're more powerful than you know, you're smarter than you know and you're more capable than you know. There are great unforeseen forces to support you on your journey here. It is true, you can survive while barely tapping into them, but if you choose to fully engage in their infinite supply, what follows is nothing short of pure magic.

About the Author: Visit www.RandiPierce.com for more information about the Life ~ By Design Formula™ and free resources to help you design your life and business for more joy, ease and abundance.

Letting the Spirit Speak

SHERRI GARRITY

*I walked into an aboriginal museum in one of Canada's national
parks this summer. The painting on the wall of the log cabin took my
breath away, because I had seen this image before.*

*It was a person, arms outstretched and hands facing upwards. He
was surrounded by pine, in a dark sky lit by dancing Northern Lights,
with a bird of prey in flight superimposed upon him.*

*I said a silent thanks to whoever watching over me had put this
here for me to see, then noted the name of the artist. A few days later I
found out the title of the painting. It was as if its message was intended
for me: Let the Spirit Speak.*

Mind Over What Mattered

A few short years ago, I was like so many women my age. I had a successful career and a nice house where I lived with my husband and young daughter. We took annual vacations and in between, hurried from one scheduled activity to the next. The last thing on my to do list was anything to do with me.

I had joined an architectural and engineering firm that was renowned world-wide. Our office was stunning – an open studio concept that met the world's highest recognized environmental stan-

211

dards. We had fresh air and could work outside on the deck with our laptops. The place buzzed with creativity and innovation. It was what I had been waiting for.

After several years in many top-down, Old Boys' Club corporate environments, I finally felt like I was part of something important. The hours and the commute were long. My husband and daughter ate many bad dinners without me. But I reasoned with myself that it was worth it. I remember telling my boss, "I feel like I can finally breathe here."

Life had other plans for me. On November 11, a national holiday in Canada, I woke up and looked forward to the long weekend. That afternoon, I began to feel chilled. A few hours later I had a high fever.

It was pneumonia, and it was the second time in five years. At home for a few weeks, I had a startling revelation. I realized that I'd rather be at home sick than at work. A few months later I became self-employed.

I was exhilarated and free. But I still didn't listen.

Early Warning Signs

I threw myself into my new business with as much passion and muscle as I had to give. I spent a lot of time strategizing and doing what I knew to do from my years in marketing. Business was great and I worked "less" than my career days but made a lot more money. I patted myself on the back. I associated with the "right" network and made an immediate splash.

I soon realized that the exterior and the interior didn't fit. Looking back, the signs of my spirit trying to get my attention were there. I remember being in the audience of an internet marketing celebrity event the first year. I went up to my swanky hotel room and sobbed. Even though my business was successful, I felt very confused and conflicted. The glitz, the high pressure sales, and especially the model of how to structure and market six and seven-figure programs felt distasteful to me. But I drank the Kool-Aid anyway.

I hired a very expensive marketing coach, cleaned out my savings to pay her, and even though in my heart, I wasn't buying what she was selling, I signed up again and again for more big ticket expenses. I tried to reconcile the vision she had for me with what my heart told me. Trying to convince myself didn't work but I chalked it up to my own fears and a normal reaction to the discomfort of "playing a bigger game".

In hindsight, it all makes sense. I made a series of choices that put me on this path. I had formed patterns of thinking about money, wealth, and the link between sacrifice and success. I had also become an expert at needing to be the best and setting my standards for myself much higher than I would expect from anyone else. The traits that drive many women entrepreneurs to succeed are also the traits that can drive us into the ground.

I had success rituals, and they worked. I lived and died by planning and deadlines. Once the strategy and the action items were set, nothing or no one could stop me from getting it done. I am highly organized, quick and able to juggle many complicated projects at one time. My husband once called me The Terminator. He's right, I don't give up, and I always get my man.

Two Life-Changing Decisions

People who knew me in my corporate past say it's like I'm a totally different person now. I believe this is true. Having my own business, one built uniquely around me and all of my strengths and weaknesses has catapulted me into territories of myself that I didn't know existed. There are mountains higher than I thought possible to climb and there are depths much deeper than I thought I could safely swim. But I am now more myself than ever.

I began to realize that even though I'd been able to get 75 percent closer to truly having a business that was 100 percent authentic and unique to me, I wasn't able to get all the way there. I wasn't holding up my end, so to speak, and the end that I was dropping, was the essence of me. The essence which is all that is left when we strip away the labels and roles we create.

I also realized that the pop-culture advice so common in entrepreneurial circles of "feeling the fear and doing it anyway" doesn't work. Feeling the fear and forcing yourself through it is worthless if the reason you fear something, is because it really isn't a fit for you. It's just another badge of false honour we wear to convince ourselves we're doing the right thing. It's the ultimate ego stroke – like the cliché of the middle-aged man buying the red convertible as a way to feel young again.

About a year ago, I made two decisions that changed my life. These decisions have become my most powerful success rituals.

I was sitting at a barnboard table looking out at the Superstition Mountains in Goldfield, Arizona. My husband and daughter were with me and we were enjoying a few days vacation after a marketing workshop in Tucson. This outdoor saloon is one of my favourite places, set in an authentic ghost town. A gentleman in full cowboy gear rode up on a gorgeous horse, tied her to the rail and ordered himself lunch and a cold beer. Never able to resist a horse, of course I had to meet her. At that moment I decided I had to find a way to have horses in my life again.

The second decision came later that week. I was in Los Angeles for another event. I felt the nagging feeling that something was not right for me. I decided that for 2010, I would give up my need to work hard, commit to trying new ways of being and not doing, and instead, find ways to live and work with grace and ease.

On the surface, these decisions seem pretty simple. But that was the key. Simple was the one thing I hadn't tried.

My Success Rituals

Working harder is not the point. Working hard at things that are easy for you isn't it either. To truly achieve success, you have to know yourself and have the courage to listen.

I still plan, I still focus, and I use my knowledge and skills, but in a different way. Now, I pull out those skills when I need them, but only after first connecting to what my inner voice tells me is right. This takes a whole different kind of work, but it always begins with awareness.

My spirit tried to tell me things when I had self doubts and a feeling that the popular model was not a fit for me. It tried to tell me for many years in my career that I wasn't in the right place. I ignored it. If you ignore it long enough, your body has a way of taking over. You'll get sick, or you'll crash. The warning signs are always there. Whether you call it your spirit, your soul, a God or the Universe, it doesn't matter. We all have an inner voice if we take the time to listen to it.

When I made the decision to find a way to have horses in my life again, I had no idea how or what this would mean. At the time I knew no one with a horse, had no contacts or current knowledge, and felt like I had forgotten all I'd learned as a child growing up with two horses of my own. But within two weeks of coming back from Arizona, I met a woman in my area who has become a lifelong friend. I started to ride her horse and hang out with two mares she rescued. Five months later I bought my own horse. I renamed him Spirit because I thought of him with that name from the moment I saw his picture.

What's happened since then has been nothing short of a spiritual, emotional and physical journey that has changed my life and my path.

1. I feel joy. The last time I remembered feeling concentrated and pure joy as an adult was the first time I heard my daughter's heartbeat. Now I feel it most days and I can call up that feeling when I need a boost.

2. I feel connection to my body. I am convinced we have lost our ability to feel. We are slaves to our minds. We have lost that awareness of our senses and our physical space in the world. We have become really good at tuning out our warning signals.

3. I feel connection to my spirit. Being with my horse forces me to listen and be aware. My horse reminds me in his body language and behavior when I am being honest and when I have clear intentions. The spirit finally gets to speak. Spirit, my horse, allows me to speak. You will have your own way to connect.

4. I feel connection to my intuition. Even though I've always had it, I didn't always listen to it. Now this is one of my most important success rituals. I have my own version of meditation and connection. You will have your own way. But quiet time and going within has enriched my life and I am convinced it is what many of us need the most.

I'm forever recovering. But just in case I forget to listen and to let my spirit speak, I get constant reminders. One of the images that came to me last year was of an eagle flying through me. I looked around. There were pine trees. The sky was dark, and lit by the Northern Lights. I watched the eagle spread its wings and fly away. I can't wait to see where it goes next.

Footnote:

I find immense power in every line of this Lakota Prayer.

Wakan Tanka, Great Mystery,

teach me how to trust

my heart,

my mind,

my intuition,

my inner knowing,

the senses of my body,

the blessings of my spirit.

Teach me to trust these things

so that I may enter my Sacred Space

and love beyond my fear,

and thus Walk in Balance

with the passing of each glorious Sun.

According to the Lakota native people, the Sacred Space is the space between exhalation and inhalation. To Walk in Balance is to have Heaven (spirituality) and Earth (physicality) in harmony.

About the Author: Sherri Garrity *is the Chief Corporate Fugitive and creator of a step-by-step system for ex-corporate employees to go from overwhelmed employee (or feeling like one) to extraordinary entrepreneur. Corporate Fugitive provides training and consulting services to show entrepreneurs how to save valuable time, energy and money by setting themselves up for success and creating custom fit businesses.*

Sherri sees the bigger picture and gets to the heart of the matter very quickly - with just the right mix of calm and reassuring presence, business and marketing wisdom, and "practical inspiration". Her style blends authenticity and business knowledge shaped by her own experience leaving a successful 20-year career in marketing and communications consulting behind. Visit www.corporatefugitive.com for business building articles and resources, and www.sherrigarrity.com to see what else Sherri is up to.

Of Creatures and Habits

SUSAN C. DAFFRON

You're a creature of habit. So am I. Just about anything you do repeatedly is destined to become a habit. Cultivating good habits can have a huge impact on your life and business. It always amazes me how many people sort of float along not realizing how what they are doing (and not doing) can affect what happens to them.

One of my favorite quotations is from Henry David Thoreau:

Go confidently in the direction of your dreams.
Live the life you imagined.

I first encountered this quote on big desk calendar I had when I was working in a cubicle. At the end of the year, I cut out the quote, and took that scrap of paper with me after I left Corporate America and started my business in 1994. The quote has been hanging on the wall of my home office ever since.

The reason this quote resonates for me is because it focuses on the fact that you and you alone are in control of what happens to you. Rather than just floating aimlessly, you can cultivate habits that help you realize your dreams.

Although my definition of success may be different than yours, I believe that certain habits can help move you toward more contentment and satisfaction in your life and business. I know the following five habits have helped me during the more than 15 years I have been in business.

1. The Work Habit

It may sound overly simplistic, but doing something (anything!) is better than doing nothing. Many people are incredibly unproductive. They spend a whole lot of time on meaningless activities and get almost nothing done. Before you start any task, think about how it is (or is not) going to move you forward in your business.

When you work, work. When you goof off, goof off. Don't try and rationalize that goofing off is actually work. Multitasking is also not a good thing. If you are getting beeps from incoming email from six email accounts, checking your Blackberry every 30 seconds, and posting to Twitter 160 times a day, you probably aren't getting any actual productive work done.

People often ask me how I have managed to write and publish 10 books in such a short period of time. The Work Habit is the reason. When I'm working, I'm actually working.

2. The Education Habit

I'm a big believer in education. Being an entrepreneur can be challenging and there's a lot to learn. I read constantly about marketing and business. With that said, because I've been online for a long time, I've also seen countless Internet "goo-roos" make what I regard as irresponsible recommendations. If someone is saying you need to mortgage your house to attend a "life-changing" program, make sure you can afford to do it at this point in your business. Odds are good, you can get 90% of the information from a free book at the library. I love my local library and almost every month, I take home a big stack of books to read; libraries are an incredibly underutilized FREE source of vast amounts of business information.

Online, don't let your emotions be swayed by hyped-up manipulative copywriting. I always advise entrepreneurs to be cautious with their finances. Business is about making money. Don't let people con you into spending more money than you feel comfortable spending for anything. Trust your gut, and know that a lot of the people you encounter online may not be quite as financially "successful" as they'd like you to believe.

3. The Golden Rule Habit

Unfortunately, common courtesy is becoming less common, particularly online. No matter what your market, businesses that last treat their customers and partners well. If you actually do what you say you're going to do when you say you're going to do it, you will stand out. It's the Golden Rule at work. Treat people as you would like to be treated. Obviously, mistakes can and will happen in business, but when they do, admit them, apologize, and try and make the person feel like he or she actually matters to you and your business. Everyone wants to feel important.

The Golden Rule is a magical thing. I know that trying to follow the Golden Rule and the fact that I have never missed a client deadline is a big part of the reason I have worked with some of my clients for more than ten years. If people believe you care, you will go far in business.

4. The Lifestyle Habit

My husband and I started our business to enable us to move away from the city to a rural area. Our log home is located in the middle of 40 acres of forest in deepest Idaho. We have a bunch of dogs, cats, and a big organic veggie garden. Of course, living out here in the middle of nowhere is not without its challenges, but we love it and don't ever want to have to move back to The Big City.

The whole reason our business exists is to support our lifestyle. So every decision we make is evaluated through what I think of as the "lifestyle filter." You can market a business in any number of ways. However some of them don't fit with the lifestyle we have worked so hard to create. For example, winter here is rough and the roads are bad. So I absolutely refuse to travel between late November and mid-April. The drive to the airport is just too scary. Knowing what I am—and am not—willing to do for my business is an important part of making smart decisions that I don't regret later.

5. The Persistence Habit

Contrary to what some people may say, being in business for yourself isn't always "sunshine and roses." Many Internet marketers are guilty of perpetrating a myth that when you own an online business, money just magically flows in without any effort. It's not true. Nothing happens without effort. Business—even an online business—requires work. You will have bad days. In fact, you may experience times when you wonder if it's all really worth it.

In business, you will fail repeatedly. You will launch services that no one likes and products no one wants. You may need to ditch or fold projects. Some clients will dislike your work. It's all okay. Stop and look around. Ask yourself, is this what I want? If your answer is no, it's time to reexamine what you're doing. The key is to do what's right for you.

As a business owner, problems and failures are all par for the course. It's not just you. We all go through it. So accept the fact that running your business will be work, and don't give up!

Follow Your Own Path

When it comes to business, you have to have the courage to follow your own path. Every day, many of us are bombarded with opportunities and choices. Should you try a new marketing tactic? Should you increase your prices? Should you outsource? What should you do first? Plus, many of us are overrun with messages about all the things we "should" be doing to get more clients, earn more money, and reach some mystical elusive state of "success."

You need to define success on your own terms. Yes, developing some of these habits might take some time, but be gentle with yourself, particularly if you're just starting out.

A business grows and evolves over time and no one gets everything "right" from the get go. Running a business isn't always easy, but it's easier to keep moving forward if you give yourself a break.

In the end, as Thoreau said, your success is really up to you:

Live the life you imagined!

About the Author: Susan Daffron, aka The Book Consultant, is the President of Logical Expressions, Inc. a book and software publishing company based in Sandpoint, Idaho. She is the author of 12 books, contributor to 4, and publisher of 10. Through her company, she helps aspiring writers become published book authors with an array of book production services, consulting, and publisher training.

Susan and her husband James Byrd call themselves "Techno-Homesteaders" because they started their business in 1995 so they could move away from the city and live a simpler life amidst the forests of rural Northern Idaho. Since 1996, the couple has lived their dream of doing work they enjoy from a place they love.

You can read about Susan at www.LogicalExpressions.com and read her publishing-related articles at www.TheBookConsultant.com.

Successful Moments to Be or Not to Be

TRICIA DYCKA

This is the story about how I discovered my passion to help others and how the hell I stayed in the zone without losing my mind. Although there were times I felt like I did lose it.

I am very familiar with the alone feeling that comes when you are trying to go after your dreams, and no one supports you. Not your family. Not your friends. Not your spouse.

The Awakening

Over three years ago, my husband and I moved to Florida from New York. Talk about culture shock! I felt like a fish out of water! While getting settled and used to the Floridian culture, I started looking for a job. While working in NY, I attempted to "be a good employee" and be satisfied, but it was no use. I was completely unfulfilled. I was tired of it all – of always being at someone else's beck and call, punching a clock, dealing with office politics. Every Sunday night I totally dreaded **Monday mornings**. A case of the Mondays? Please, that was everyday!

I decided that this was no way to live. It was time for something different. But what?

To figure out what was missing from my life, I started being aware of what was around me. I let go of my expectations of what should be and who I should be. I could see the world without blinders on for the first time in my life. From my observations, it became apparent that business owners and entrepreneurs were making their own choices about how to live their lives. They seemed in control and to be living out their passion.

That got me to think: if they can do it, why can't I? Oh, how I loved the thought of being able to make choices based on what I wanted. I dreamed of **living freely and enjoying life**. I had no idea how to make this change, or what business I would start. However, I knew to my core that being in charge of my time and my life made me feel like I was on top of the world.

My Plummet Back to Earth

In my naive excitement, I told my husband and our family that I was going to start my own business. I believed that they would be jumping up and down for joy like I was – like kids on Christmas morning. But that isn't what happened. Instead of jumping and hugs, there was a stunning lack of support. Our parents responded with an empty and unconvincing, "Hope it works out for you"; "You know owning your own business is very difficult". Siblings and friends "yes'd" me to death. On the surface, they were supportive, but I could hear them saying to themselves, "What is she thinking? Who would go to her? She has no experience."

I was stunned. Mentally I was sarcastically thanking them for the vote of confidence. It seemed everyone had concluded that failure was imminent for me, before I even did anything. I got the verbal equivalent of the pat on the head a child would receive when she tells her disbelieving mother that she was going to be President of the United States.

The Meltdown

Dejected and feeling alone, I set out on my entrepreneurial journey.

I was burning the candle at ends, building my business and maintaining a façade, I was fine with the lack of support. In actuality, I was in **WAY over my head**. At every turn I felt like I was being pulled deeper into a hole by some imaginary riptide. I felt I was making no progress, in business or life. I started to ask myself the same questions everyone else was asking.

- Wouldn't it be easier to just get a job?
- Have a steady paycheck?
- Why couldn't I be like everyone else?

The stress from all this led to heartburn. I felt totally defeated and unsupported. I wanted to stick my head in the sand and ignore it all. I started walking around like a zombie. Basically, I had a meltdown.

I isolated myself and stopped talking to those closest to me. Why? They made me feel crappy and I was so not interested in their two cents about how I was doing my life wrong. I began to doubt myself and my abilities.

The thought of ignoring my dream and getting a job for the next thirty years made my stomach hurt, but this emotional pit was no way to live either. It was time to make a major decision: **Do I squash what I want to do and make others happy or do I make myself happy?**

It was time for me to find out who I was and be happy from within. *To celebrate me.* I felt free.

The Other Side

From that time I spent feeling unsupported and lost, one of my key realizations was that most people are not willing to do what it takes to go after their dreams. Instead of living their dreams, people live in a bubble of false security and ridicule and pass judgment on the daring ones who are willing to risk it all.

What do I have that supports me and creates an environment where I am raring to go? What are the things that help me to stay positive and focused especially in times where I feel like I am ready to throw my hands up in the air and say F it.

First thing I did was get involved with social media and meeting some of the most wonderful, supportive, enthusiastic, energized, positive like minded peeps that I have ever had the pleasure to meet. From that we have paired into different groups that suit our personal and business needs. This alone has been the biggest step towards my success. Without that support there is a constant struggle. When I first decided to be my own boss and entrepreneur, I stumbled more times than I care to think about and quite a few times I was ready to give up.

I have had tremendous results with both accountability and collaboration partners. I became involved with a yearlong group program and out of that came my collaboration partners. These women brainstorm ideas about our businesses. We discuss ideas on marketing, new programs, how to be more efficient with the running of our businesses. We are there to motivate and cheer each other on as well as share our experience and wisdom.

My accountability partners (love them and have a few) speak once a week to every other week via phone, skype or email and we schedule what it is that we are working on and want to accomplish. We have check ins to make sure that we are on time and if not what is the issue. Sometimes it is the little voice in our head beating us up about anything or everything and we can all relate to the amount of abuse that little voice wants to dish out. Or a possible business challenge that has been made into a mountain instead of the molehill that it really is.

One thing that inhibits us from moving forward is fear. Having that accountability partner really helps to stay focused and address what is right in front of us instead of in our head. One thing I have learned on this path is that I believed I was all alone in what I was feeling and the obstacles that I was encountering. Then I started to reach out to others who have their own business and realized it is not just me going through this. It really boils down to how we handle it.

We put in a lot of hours, days, nights and weekends. It is important to know it's not just you doing it. Shedding blood, sweat and tears and the ability to know that we can pick up the phone and call someone who will support us or cry with us is amazing.

A great resource to share is meetup.com. This is a site where I go to find people with the same interests or areas that I would like to learn more about. I am involved in a Reiki meetup because it interests me. I have met some great people face to face, even though we are in a huge online era it is just as beneficial to meet people and go for coffee. Creating an offline community is just as important and empowering for our success.

I remember asking myself one day what did I do that changed my circumstances. I am going to share with you the **6 steps** that I did then and continue to do now. It has helped me tremendously. It keeps me positive and helps me when I stumble and fall flat on my face. Where the question comes in do I stand up one more time? My hope is that by sharing this with you it will help you to be able to also stand up one more time despite the negativity that may surround you. Your belief in yourself will prevail.

Step 1- Discovering what my true likes, passions, dreams were without the influence of anybody else. I got to know me and what I truly wanted to accomplish and how I could be of service. This will always be changing and evolving. I wanted to figure out who I really was without the expectations of what everyone else thought I SHOULD be doing. This is really big for a lot of people who are so accustomed to being lead by what makes others happy. It is very liberating and one of the best things I ever did and continue to do.

Step 2- Questioning all my beliefs and assumptions and I couldn't believe how much I reacted out of mechanical behaviors. Once I started to become aware of my reactions I started asking myself Is this really how I felt? Is there another way of looking at this? My favorite question to myself is WHY? A lot of what I did was start reading blogs, books and listening to the "gurus" so that I could get different perspectives from others. It has challenged me in ways I had not thought possible. Some of my favorites are Ariel and Shya Kane, Napoleon Hill, Ittybiz, and many others. Go out there and see what works for you. If you find that a certain belief no longer holds true for you drop it like a hot potato and move on.

Step 3- Engaging in the moment and truly listening to others. We all think we are great listeners, well I thought I was too until I realized and never let anyone finish speaking without already finishing the conversation in my own head. How thoughtful is that? I would have all kinds of comments and itching to jump in before they were even done with their sentence. Forget it if something they said did not agree with what I felt to be true. This one was a bit difficult for me and occasionally I still catch myself doing it. However it is a learned skill and the amount of information I have picked up from others is enormous.

Step 4- Using open communication or I feel statements which have enhanced all of my relationships. *"To effectively communicate, we must realize that we are all different in the way we perceive the world* *and use this understanding as a guide to our communication with others."* – Anthony Robbins

Sometimes it is difficult to hear when others criticize but if an open mind can be kept, a lot can be learned within these conversations. Addressing problems with others instead of harboring resentments can clear away a lot of the conflict and injured feeling.

Step 5- Creating boundaries that honor and respect us and our values. This has really helped me to stop the drama and BS coming from others as well as allowing myself to be drawn in. Learning to set boundaries is a way to become friends with ourselves, knowing we matter, and taking care of ourselves.

By defining what our needs, feelings, opinions and rights are and becoming skilled at assertively taking care of ourselves in relationships has helped me really step up and become my own person. My confidence and belief in myself has soared to new heights.

Step 6- Challenge the status quo of my environment and those in my circle as well as myself. The Comfort Zone is our living, work, and social environments that we have grown accustom to.

If someone would have told me three years ago I would be teaching classes, creating videos etc. I would have laughed.

When you do something that you previously thought impossible, you can break through barriers in other areas of life. Although you might have remarkable experiences, whether or not they become transformative is not a given, but a choice. *Step beyond the familiar and try something new!*

When we face our fears we become individuals with more diversity and understanding of how the world works.

"Do the thing you fear and the death of fear is certain." – Ralph Waldo Emerson

Anytime I feel out of alignment, it's that sinking feeling in my gut which drives me back to these 6 steps to see where I am out. Did

I get involved in a project that really wasn't right for me? Am I hanging around someone who says all the right things but doesn't walk the talk? I go within and find out where I made the wrong turn. It's not a big deal; it is only a minor course correction.

I do what I feel is the best for me. I stay upbeat because I love life. It is a big adventure! You never know what is around the corner. It may not always be what I thought or expected but there is always a choice in how I respond. My success is learning something new every day, being true to myself and expressing this in whatever way works best for me. May your journey be filled with fun, laughter, good health, friends, family and whatever you feel is best for you.

About the Author: Tricia Dycka is very familiar with the alone feeling that comes when you are trying to go after your dreams, and no one supports you. Not your family. Not your friends. Not even your significant other. She is driven to help other "lonelypreneurs" create supportive environments for themselves.

Join Tricia for Drinks Poolside and get Tips / Recipes on how to handle the negativity & Naysayers in your life. www.TriciaDycka.com

Free Gifts from the Success Rituals 2.0 Co-Authors

... a Virtual Goodie Bag to boost your success!

To celebrate the launch of this book and to thank YOU for stepping inside with us we've put together a generous collection of EXCLUSIVE tools and resources for success-driven women in business online.

Exclusive means they aren't available elsewhere for free. And, you don't have to subscribe to each one individually either. One opt-in will give you immediate access to the entire compilation of downloads.

You'll get excited when you see everything inside!

Go to www.SuccessRitualsGifts.com

and claim your free gifts now.

CPSIA information can be obtained at www.ICGtesting.com

263488BV00005B/7/P